MW00910218

AppleTalk® Network
System Overview

Addison-Wesley Publishing Company, Inc.

Reading, Massachusetts ∎ Menlo Park, California ∎ New York
Don Mills, Ontario ∎ Wokingham, England ∎ Amsterdam ∎ Bonn
Sydney ∎ Singapore ∎ Tokyo ∎ Madrid ∎ San Juan

Writers: Keri Wagner, Paul Goode

Designer: Lisa Mirski

Art Directors: Deborah Dennis, Li Greiner, Joyce Zavarro

Editors: Paul Dreyfus, Amy Satran

Production Editor: Charlotte Clark

Technical Advisor: Rich Andrews

Illustrator: Al McCahon

Concept: Becky Howard

Contents

3 Network Services, Maintenance, and Applications / 27

Part II   AppleTalk Protocols and Their Application

Figures and tables

Part II   AppleTalk Protocols and Their Application

CHAPTER 4   **AppleTalk Protocols 59**

Preface

The *AppleTalk® Network System Overview* provides a technical introduction to the AppleTalk network system and Apple Computer's approach to networking in order to encourage the development of new applications.

So that it may be useful to a variety of readers, the book offers:

- an historical review of the key goals and development of the AppleTalk network system

- descriptions of the components and features of an AppleTalk network system

- a brief guide to administering an AppleTalk network system

- an overview of the AppleTalk protocol architecture and brief introductions of each of the protocols

- thorough cross referencing to other Apple® publications that describe the specifics of each product

The book is a useful source of information about the functionality of Apple's networking products, and will help readers make informed decisions about product purchases and implementations as well as the development of new products.

The book's audience and organization

The *AppleTalk Network System Overview* is aimed at a range of readers. Although intended primarily to allow developers to gain an overview of Apple's approach to computer networking, the book also contains information that will be useful to information systems managers, network administrators, and others in business or education seeking knowledge about how the AppleTalk network system can meet their networking needs.

Part I familiarizes readers with the history of AppleTalk and the features of an AppleTalk network system. The material is relevant to all readers interested in exploring an AppleTalk network's capabilities, although it's neither a tutorial nor a networking primer. (Readers looking for a basic introduction to networks should see *Understanding Computer Networks*, another book in the Apple Communications Library.) Chapter 1 introduces the reader to AppleTalk, explaining why it was developed and highlighting its unique features; it serves as a platform upon which is then built an understanding of networking products (Chapter 2) and, next, the services made available to AppleTalk network users and the methods used to administer an AppleTalk network (Chapter 3).

Part II describes the inner workings of an AppleTalk network system. Chapters 4 and 5 contain a technical overview of the AppleTalk protocols and the application of these protocols in the Macintosh® computer's AppleTalk Manager. The chapters also provide basic information on the functionality of each protocol; developers looking for detailed specifications of the protocols should consult the Apple Communications Library volume *Inside AppleTalk*.

The book's two appendixes consist of a guide to other Apple publications about its networking products, and the guidelines developers of applications should follow when they work on products for international distribution. The glossary defines terms used throughout the book.

Terminology and conventions

This book uses several terms in a general manner:

- Macintosh: Any Macintosh computer, which includes all models unless stated otherwise

- Apple II: an Apple IIe or IIGS® computer

- PC: any personal computer that is 100 percent compatible with the IBM Personal Computer.

A new term in this book is printed in bold type. This indicates that the term is defined in the glossary.

Associated documents

In addition to presenting original information, the *AppleTalk Network System Overview* condenses material from several detailed networking and communications documents and other Apple publications. Appendix A, the guide to related Apple publications, identifies the documents that have been drawn upon in this book and describes the primary audience and contents of each.

Part I AppleTalk Hardware and Software

Chapter 1 An Introduction to AppleTalk

BY THE END OF 1983, personal computer developers had begun to admit that realizing the vast potential of computer networking had proved elusive. While the promise was great, acceptance was slower than expected. Several factors had contributed; connection to a network system was expensive and the resulting services were few. More importantly, it seemed that the network user had been ignored: rather than developing networks as tools to extend the user's reach, designers focused on technology for its own sake. Thus, issues such as data transmission speed seemed to take on a greater significance than user convenience or cost. Users found that they had to access network resources differently than the resources on their personal computers. Networks, it appeared, had become a hindrance.

At the same time, Apple Computer, Inc. was preparing to introduce the first Macintosh® computer. This computer would revolutionize the idea of usability, establishing a new standard for the interface between the personal computer and the personal computer user. As Apple engineers evaluated ways in which they might connect Macintosh computers through a network, they agreed that their design must seamlessly extend the user's computing experience to the network and that the design must ultimately be independent of any one computer. They elected to innovate freely where necessary, but to develop an architecture that would utilize standard technology where appropriate. This architecture became the foundation of the AppleTalk® network system. ∎

Computer network systems are the basis of distributed computing. They make it possible for computer users to communicate and to share resources despite the presence of barriers of location and distance. Physically, these systems consist of computing components joined by connectivity components. Computing devices (such as personal computers, minicomputers, and mainframe computers) and special server devices (such as file servers and mail servers) are connected via a variety of cables, other data channels, and routing and gateway components. When they have access to a network system, computer users can communicate with one another, gather and exchange information, and share printing and file storage resources.

Key goals of the AppleTalk network system

As Apple engineers discussed and debated the potential of networking Macintosh computers, several architectural themes became apparent to them. First of all, although the initial use of the AppleTalk network system would be by Macintosh users, the system needed to be versatile enough to accommodate many different kinds of computers and other devices. Thus, it was determined that the AppleTalk network system should incorporate a range extending from the attachment of a few peripheral devices to a single Macintosh computer all the way to an internetwork connecting thousands of computer systems dispersed across a wide geographical area. This meant recognizing that network technology should allow users to exchange and share information without concern for the special format and internal idiosyncrasies of dissimilar computer systems. The AppleTalk network system, then, must allow any type of computer to participate as an equal—and to the best of its ability.

Because they were, at least initially, dealing with a computer of modest size and memory, the engineers agreed that the underlying protocol architecture should be simple and easy to implement. (A complicated architecture would require complicated devices.) It was also clear that they should adopt a "plug-and-play" capability, wherein the user could plug a computing device into a network system and use it immediately, without any of the complications of configuration.

Moreover, the network system's architecture should avoid centralized control, which would increase the initial entry cost of the system and create a single point of failure. Instead, the architecture must be peer-to-peer, under which any device on the network could communicate with any other without going through a host-provided service.

A fourth, and critical, architectural decision posited that the protocol architecture must remain open. Since the designers couldn't predict all of the things that people would want to do with the network, this would leave open the possibilities for future development.

A consequence of an open architecture was the idea of link independence. By remaining independent of the physical link that connected computer devices, AppleTalk allows the introduction of other technologies without the major costs of redesigning the protocol architecture and refitting ROMs and system software. Today, for example, DuPont fiber optic, Ethernet, and LANSTAR cablings can all be used in an AppleTalk network system.

Finally, the developers agreed, the AppleTalk network system must stand as a seamless extension of the user's computer. This meant that access to network resources should not be achieved through foreign and complicated means. In particular, the Desktop Interface of the Macintosh would be maintained across the network system. By making this commitment, the AppleTalk designers ensured that, to the user, access to and use of the network would be a natural extension of the access and use of their personal computer. Since network resources could then be obtained in the same manner as local resources, the AppleTalk network system would succeed in truly extending the user's reach.

The AppleTalk network system

The fulfillment of these key goals resulted in AppleTalk, a comprehensive network system that today is used by an installed base of more than 1.5 million computers and servers in networks that range in size from a minimum of two devices to large internets with thousands of devices.

Although the initial installation of AppleTalk was spurred on by a trio of products—the Macintosh computer, the LaserWriter® printer, and LocalTalk™ connectivity—today it can connect a variety of computers and peripherals via several data transmission media. This versatility of design has allowed network managers to choose, for example, transmission media to meet specific needs, such as cost, expected traffic flow, speed, noise resistance, and ease of installation. As such, AppleTalk enables communication between network devices (including users' computers, file servers, and printers) which may be a *mixture* of Apple® and non-Apple products.

Several elements make up an AppleTalk network system: AppleTalk software—which runs in each device connected to the system and observes the AppleTalk protocols—and AppleTalk hardware. The latter includes computing components and connectivity components.

AppleTalk protocol architecture

The devices on a network system interact according to carefully designed and scrupulously enforced rules of interplay called **protocols.** Internal descriptions of a network system consist mainly of discussion and specification of the protocols, their objectives, and their interactions. Collectively, this information is called the protocol architecture of the network system.

AppleTalk protocols are arranged in layers (see *Figure 1-1*); each protocol draws upon the services of other protocol(s) and delivers an enhanced service to either some other protocol or to an application. Thus, a protocol in a higher layer secures services from one or more protocols in the lower layers. Figure 1-1 provides a framework for examining the interaction of the different protocols and for isolating functionality to certain portions of the architecture. This structure allows a divide-and-conquer approach to designing and building the protocol architecture.

Layered models for network protocols are inspired by their earlier use in describing various concepts (in particular, operating systems) of stand-alone computers. Today, most carefully designed network systems rely on a layered protocol architecture. *Inside AppleTalk,* another book in the Apple Communications Library, contains the definitive description of the AppleTalk protocol architecture and a detailed specification of the AppleTalk protocols; an overview of the architecture appears in Chapter 4 of this book.

AppleTalk hardware

The network devices and cabling methods comprise the physical or hardware components of an AppleTalk network system. The layout of a network is called its **topology**, that is, the arrangement of the devices and cables of the network system (see *Figure 1-2*).

AppleTalk's design allows users to include a wide variety of data transmission **media**. Current widely used transmission media include LocalTalk, EtherTalk™, and LANSTAR AppleTalk from Northern Telecom, which are all described in Chapter 2. (EtherTalk uses standard Ethernet media and LANSTAR AppleTalk uses Meridian LANSTAR media.) These different links can be interconnected in the AppleTalk system via routers to build very large local or geographically dispersed internets. The user can evaluate expected traffic, distance, cost and desired response characteristics in a given portion of the internet and choose a link accordingly. Also, wide-area links (such as telephone lines) can extend the geographical reach of an AppleTalk network.

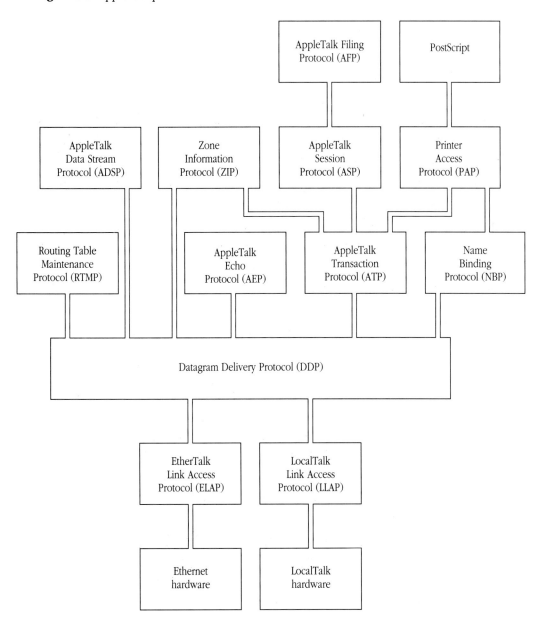

■ **Figure 1-2** Topology: The layout of a network

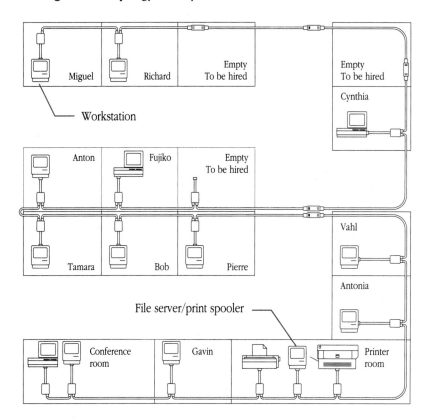

AppleTalk services

We have seen that AppleTalk, using diverse media, may unite an arbitrarily large number of devices across a vast area, while at the same time meeting its goal of providing a seamless extension of the user's computer. But AppleTalk is more than a relatively transparent means of extending the physical reach of a personal computer. Ultimately, it was designed as a foundation for interpersonal computing and to stand as a fundamental improvement in the way people use personal computers. This is demonstrated by the presence of two examples of end-user services developed for this purpose: shared printing and shared filing.

Shared printing means that a printer on the network can be shared by multiple personal computers. The most straightforward version of shared printing is called direct printing. Here, a computer sends a print job directly to a printer connected to the network. AppleTalk also supports printing with a **print spooler,** which is a hardware or software application that interacts with a printer to print documents. When a computer sends a file to be printed, the print spooler intercepts the file and handles all printer interaction, freeing the computer for other tasks. In an AppleTalk network system, shared printing can be handled by an AppleShare® **print server.** A detailed discussion of shared printing appears in Chapter 3.

Shared filing provides a common platform so that information can be shared across dissimilar computers. Beyond that, it enables network users to store and gain access to common files without disrupting other users' activities. A tier of access privileges controls the degree of sharing, limiting the availability of a file to a single user or to a selected group of users. Within an AppleTalk network system, an AppleShare **file server** provides a location for this activity. Shared filing is also covered in Chapter 3.

Computing and connectivity components

Again, a significant AppleTalk design goal focused on versatility: that is, although the development of AppleTalk was directed at the Macintosh, AppleTalk needed ultimately to allow any type of computer to participate as an equal. Moreover, the designers believed, the network system itself should be expandable enough to connect a large number of devices across physical and geographical barriers.

Besides the Macintosh, many other popular computers are connected to AppleTalk systems, notably the Apple IIe and Apple IIGs® computers, the PC family developed by International Business Machines Corporation, PC compatibles, Digital Equipment Corporation's VAX™ computers, and a variety of UNIX® computers. These computers attach to AppleTalk in different ways. For example, an Apple IIe computer requires an Apple II Workstation Card, while an Apple IIGs has LocalTalk hardware built in and requires no extra hardware. IBM PCs participate by using special hardware and software, namely the LocalTalk PC Card and driver and AppleShare PC software.

AppleTalk for VMS™ software is a complete implementation of AppleTalk protocols for the VAX computer's VMS operating environment. Within this environment, the VAX computer functions as a virtual AppleTalk network joined to another AppleTalk network with a router application running on the VAX. That is, a VAX process becomes functionally equivalent to a node on an AppleTalk internet, and appears that way to other devices on the internet. With AppleTalk for VMS comes the connectivity needed to create and run applications distributed between a

VAX/VMS system and other computers. The software includes a programming interface for developing applications and services on a VAX.

The mixture of peripherals connected to AppleTalk systems has expanded far beyond the LaserWriter. AppleTalk networks typically support ImageWriter® printers, very high resolution printers, modem servers, and several other peripherals, servers, and gateways.

The volume and complexity of connectivity solutions has grown past LocalTalk to encompass the various media already discussed here, as well as phone lines and dial-up access. (Dial-up access allows a remote connection from a single machine to a network through the telephone system. For example, it permits a user to access an office network from a home computer and obtain all available services. The home computer then functions as though it were a device on the office network.)

Local area networks and internets

On a **local area network (LAN),** computer users exchange information and share printers, file servers, modems, and other resources over short distances, such as within an office. (See *Figure 1-3*). A single network using LocalTalk cabling can connect up to 32 nodes. (A **node** is, simply, any device connected to the network, such as a personal computer or file server.)

■ **Figure 1-3** Local area network

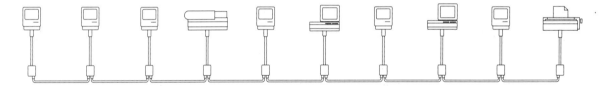

At its most elemental, an **internet** consists of two or more local area networks linked together with a router or gateway. When a **router** combines network segments into an internet (see *Figure 1-4*), the component networks remain independent of each other. The router handles information forwarding throughout the internet. The nodes connected to an internet can function either as members of their original local area network or as part of the new internet. When routers are used to form internets, the networks in the internet are usually regrouped into **zones.** A zone is a logical grouping of networks on an internet. A network's zone need not be related to its physical location, although all networks in a zone must reside on the same internet.

When many local area networks form an internet, a **backbone** can be used to ease cross-network traffic congestion, which may occur when nodes on one network need to send data to nodes on other networks and must go through several routers to reach the destination network. With a well-planned backbone network, data from nodes on a local area network can be sent through a minimal number of routers to reach the destination network.

■ **Figure 1-4**   AppleTalk internet

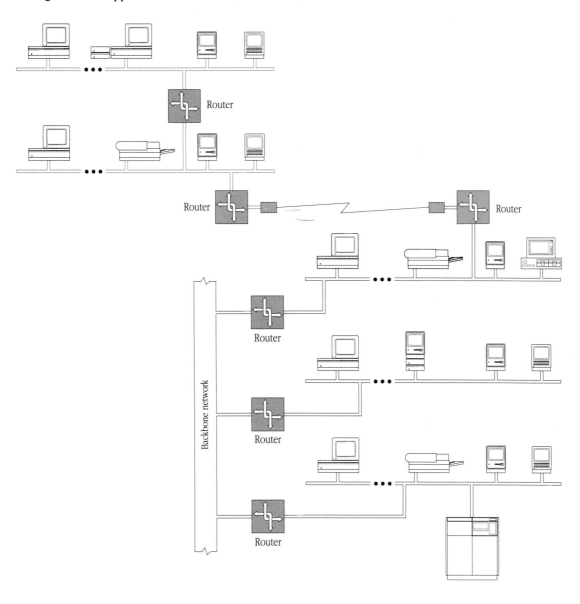

The AppleTalk network system: A review

So far, we've reviewed AppleTalk in the context of its historical framework: how it was developed, the original goals set for it, and how those goals are evidenced in practice. Chapter 2 discusses different AppleTalk connectivity products, starting with a look at the different types of physical connection methods, then specifically addressing the features and hardware of LocalTalk, EtherTalk, and LANSTAR AppleTalk.

Chapter 2 **AppleTalk Connectivity Products**

AN APPLETALK NETWORK SYSTEM is a collection of computers
and intelligent peripheral devices that communicate using AppleTalk
protocols over some medium to which they are all connected. AppleTalk
networks can be connected with a variety of media, each of which provides
the physical link required for network devices to exchange information.

Three products that can be used to provide connectivity in an AppleTalk
network are LocalTalk, EtherTalk, and LANSTAR AppleTalk. This chapter
discusses these products and the hardware and software required to use each
of them. ∎

Communicating over different media

A *protocol family* is a collection of related protocols that together enable communication over a network. For example, the combination of all AppleTalk protocols is an example of a protocol family. A *protocol stack* is an implementation of a particular protocol family within a node.

The two lowest layers of a protocol architecture are the data link — or link access — layer, which handles the delivery of data between nodes and the physical layer, which includes the cables, connectors and hardware that controls transmission and reception. Within the AppleTalk protocol architecture, the **LocalTalk Link Access Protocol (LLAP)** is a commonly-used data link layer protocol that manages the delivery of packets over LocalTalk cabling. However, LocalTalk cabling is not required in AppleTalk. To run AppleTalk over different media, other link access protocols and hardware can be substituted for LLAP and LocalTalk.

The link access protocols used with LocalTalk, Ethernet, and Meridian LANSTAR cabling are all different, but they provide the same services to the higher-layer protocols above them. These higher-layer protocols are unaffected when, for example, the **EtherTalk Link Access Protocol (ELAP)** and Ethernet hardware are substituted for LLAP and LocalTalk. AppleTalk protocols can be run over a variety of physical links.

A single node may be connected at the same time to several different networks, each employing different link access protocols and physical hardware. This is possible in a Macintosh **workstation**, for example, although currently, AppleTalk packets can only be sent and received through a single link access protocol at any one time. (Routers are special devices in that they can simultaneously transmit and receive on multiple links.) The Macintosh **LAP Manager** software directs AppleTalk protocol information through the appropriate link access protocol (see *Figure 4-3*).

Different data link protocols may use different schemes for addressing nodes. These addressing schemes may differ from those employed by higher-layer protocols, requiring some means to reconcile the two. The **AppleTalk Address Resolution Protocol (AARP)** reconciles addressing discrepancies between a data link protocol and the rest of a protocol family. For example, AARP resolves the differences between the AppleTalk addressing scheme and the Ethernet addressing scheme, allowing transport of encapsulated AppleTalk data over an Ethernet data link.

Cable selection

Careful selection of the cable type is an essential part of the network installation process. Within an AppleTalk network system, many different types of media can be used. The appropriate cable type depends on the system's requirements and projected needs.

Factors to consider when choosing a transmission medium include bandwidth, noise resistance, attenuation, cost, ease of installation, and building codes. **Bandwidth** is a measure of the cable's transmission capacity, which is usually measured in bits per second (bps). **Noise resistance** is the cable's ability to keep signals free of distortion and outside interference. **Attenuation** is the weakening of signals over distance.

Twisted-pair cable consists of two wires that are individually insulated and then twisted together. The twisted pair is then covered with an insulation jacket (see *Figure 2-1*).

LocalTalk cable is one example of twisted-pair cable, as is the cable used with telephone systems. LANSTAR networks also use twisted-pair cable. Generally, twisted-pair cable is inexpensive and easy to install. However, it usually has a lower bandwidth and may be susceptible to noise interference.

Coaxial cable is made up of an inner conducting wire surrounded by an outer conductor (see *Figure 2-1*). Between the inner and outer conductors is an insulating layer, and the entire cable may be shielded to keep out noise.

Coaxial cable is usually more expensive, both to buy and install, than twisted-pair cable, but its higher bandwidth usually permits faster transmission. Also, its outer shield helps reduce noise and other interference. EtherTalk, for example, uses Ethernet coaxial cable.

The boundaries between ratings for different media are being blurred by continuing advances in media technology. For example, techniques for transmitting at high speed over twisted-pair wiring have become available, enabling this media type to be used for 10 Mbps Ethernet transmissions.

■ **Figure 2-1** Twisted-pair and coaxial cable

Twisted-pair cable

Coaxial cable

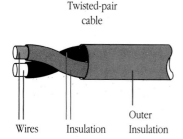

Wires   Insulation   Outer Insulation

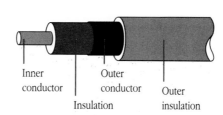

Inner conductor   Outer conductor   Insulation   Outer insulation

LocalTalk

LocalTalk is an inexpensive, easy means of linking workstations and peripheral devices in an AppleTalk network system. The hardware consists of cables, connectors, and cable extenders. LocalTalk is ideal for small, local work groups where moderate data transfer rates are acceptable.

LocalTalk twisted-pair cable supports a maximum of 32 devices and allows transmission speeds of up to 230.4 kilobits per second (Kbps). A LocalTalk network can span up to a total of 1000 feet. Connector kits contain the hardware necessary for linking a node to the network (see *Figure 2-2*). Each connector kit includes

■ a LocalTalk connector module

■ a two-meter LocalTalk cable with locking connector

■ a LocalTalk cable extender

■ the *LocalTalk Cable System Owner's Guide*

A **connector module** is a small box with a cable attached to it that connects the node to the LocalTalk cables.

The LocalTalk connector module may be terminated by either a mini-circular 8-pin, or 9-pin plug. An 8-pin mini-circular plug is used with the Apple IIe, Apple IIGS, Macintosh Plus, Macintosh SE, and Macintosh II computers, the LaserWriter IINT and LaserWriter IINTX printers, and the ImageWriter II printer with the LocalTalk option. A 9-pin plug is needed for the Macintosh 128K, 512K, and Macintosh 512K enhanced computers, and the LaserWriter and LaserWriter Plus printers.

A **cable extender** is an adapter that joins two cables. LocalTalk cable comes in 10- and 25-meter lengths. An authorized Apple dealer can provide information on available cabling kits.

■ **Figure 2-2** LocalTalk connector kit

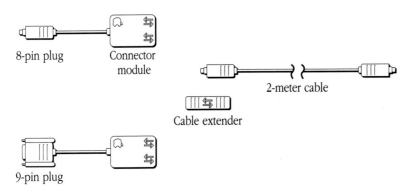

8-pin plug   Connector module

2-meter cable

Cable extender

9-pin plug

Since a **transceiver** for transmitting and receiving information over LocalTalk is built into every Macintosh and Apple IIGS computer, as well as the LaserWriter printer and other peripheral devices, setting up the network is simply a matter of physically connecting the devices (see *Figure 2-3*).

■ **Figure 2-3** LocalTalk network

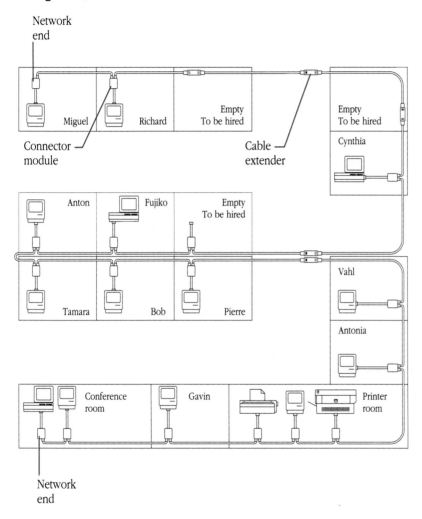

The **bus topology** and connector modules allow easy expansion of the network. Adding a device to the end of the network involves plugging in a cable and a connector module without interrupting network service (see *Figure 2-4*).

■ **Figure 2-4** Adding a device to the end of a LocalTalk network

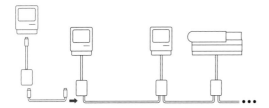

Adding a device between existing network devices requires temporarily disrupting the network, but the process is the same: adding cable and a connector module, if necessary, and then plugging in the device. Removing a device requires simply unplugging the device from its connector module. The connector module may remain on the network indefinitely without having a device attached to it.

EtherTalk

Apple's EtherTalk product permits AppleTalk network protocols to run on high-speed Ethernet coaxial cable. This high-bandwidth medium is preferable for networks that carry heavy traffic or have workstations connected over longer distances.

EtherTalk implementations support up to 254 active AppleTalk users on a network with up to 1023 total devices. Thick (standard) Ethernet cable allows a maximum of 200 nodes per 1640-foot segment, with 8202 feet the maximum network length. Thin Ethernet cable allows 30 nodes per 656-foot segment over a maximum network length of 3281 feet.

EtherTalk allows data transmission speeds of up to 10 megabits per second (Mbps), significantly higher than the speed of LocalTalk. Either thick Ethernet or thin Ethernet cables may be used; both must be configured in a bus topology. EtherTalk manages data flow so it can coexist on Ethernet cable with other non-AppleTalk protocols. An EtherTalk network is often part of an internet that includes LocalTalk networks (see *Figure 2-5*).

Linking LocalTalk and EtherTalk networks enhances the functionality offered by using only one or the other. For one, LaserWriter printers and ImageWriter printers with the AppleTalk option must connect to a LocalTalk network; Ethernet users can gain access to these printers only if the EtherTalk network is joined to a LocalTalk network. On the other hand, an AppleTalk network can benefit by using a high-bandwidth Ethernet backbone, which can increase data transmission rates.

■ **Figure 2-5** AppleTalk internet using an Ethernet backbone network

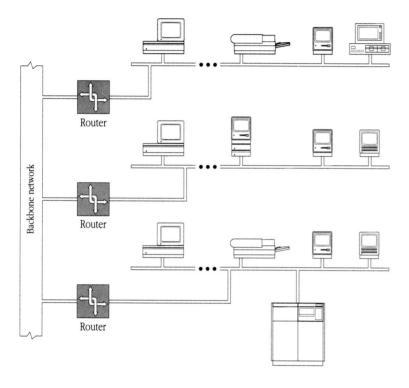

EtherTalk for the Macintosh II (or Macintosh IIx) is an alternative connectivity option for AppleTalk and requires:

■ an EtherTalk Interface Card

■ the *EtherTalk Installer for the Macintosh Operating System* disk

■ an installed network of Ethernet cable

Each Macintosh II workstation needs an EtherTalk Interface Card and the EtherTalk software installed. Note that any Macintosh computer can operate EtherTalk software as long as it has a compatible Ethernet interface card and driver, or some other connection device installed.

This document does not specifically address Ethernet cabling and protocols. For more information refer to *The Ethernet—A Local Area Network: Data Link Layer and Physical Layer Specifications* (Ethernet Blue Book) from Xerox Corporation.

EtherTalk software

EtherTalk software for the Macintosh family enables data transmission and reception over Ethernet cable. The software contains:

■ Control Panel software

■ the LAP Manager and its INIT Resource

■ the AppleTalk Address Resolution Protocol implementation

■ the Ethernet driver

Control Panel software

The Network control device package of the Control Panel software (its network 'cdev') displays the icons that represent each possible connection to a network. For example, on a Macintosh with EtherTalk installed, the Control Panel would show an icon for built-in LocalTalk and an icon for EtherTalk (see *Figure 2-6*).

■ **Figure 2-6** Control Panel

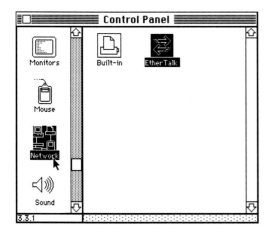

The Control Panel software searches the System Folder for all alternative AppleTalk connection files ('adev's). The Control Panel then displays the icons for these connections, and the user can select the connection to use. A workstation can use only one AppleTalk network connection at a time, although it may be connected physically to several networks, such as a LocalTalk network and an EtherTalk network. The workstation sends and receives data via the selected network connection only.

LAP Manager

An interface to the data link layer, the LAP Manager directs encapsulated data, called **packets,** to the appropriate AppleTalk connection. For example, in a Macintosh connected to the AppleTalk network by LocalTalk and EtherTalk, the LAP Manager sends packets to the connection selected in the Control Panel. The LAP Manager standardizes interactions between link access protocol implementations and the higher-level protocol implementations.

The actual implementation code for an alternate AppleTalk selection is held in an area called the 'atlk' resource within the 'adev' file. The 'atlk' resource makes all calls to the LAP Manager, telling the LAP Manager which AppleTalk implementation is active and how to handle incoming and outgoing packets. See the Apple publication *EtherTalk and Alternate AppleTalk Connections Reference* for complete information on the LAP Manager.

AARP and EtherTalk

The AppleTalk Address Resolution Protocol maps between any two sets of data link layer addresses. For example, to allow AppleTalk protocols to be used on Ethernet cable, the AARP implementation used by EtherTalk maps between a 48-bit address required by Ethernet and an 8-bit address required by AppleTalk. The Ethernet address, also called the **hardware address,** is determined by the physical and data link protocols of the network. The AppleTalk address, also called the **protocol address,** is the node address used by higher-level AppleTalk protocols.

AARP performs three basic functions:

■ initial determination of a unique protocol address for a given protocol client

■ mapping from a protocol address to a hardware address

■ filtering of packets for a protocol address

In a single node, there may be more than one protocol **client** and more than one link access protocol implementation. For each link access protocol a node recognizes, AARP maintains a collection of protocol addresses and their corresponding hardware addresses. These addresses are kept in an **address mapping table (AMT).**

From AARP's point of view, a node may encounter two types of packets on a network: data and AARP packets. Data packets contain information for a link access protocol to process. AARP packets perform address-resolution functions.

In EtherTalk's implementation of AARP, a data packet contains a 14-byte header that identifies the Ethernet destination address and Ethernet source address, which are both hardware addresses, and the Ethernet protocol type (see *Figure 2-7*). For AppleTalk protocol packets, the Ethernet protocol type is $809B (a $ preceding a number indicates a hexadecimal value). Following the header is the AppleTalk packet, which contains a 3-byte header specifying the AppleTalk destination address and source address, which are both protocol addresses, and the type, followed by the link access data field.

The minimum acceptable size of Ethernet data packets is 60 bytes. Thus, smaller packets must be padded to at least 60 bytes. The maximum size allowed for an AppleTalk packet on Ethernet is 617 bytes, including the Ethernet header.

■ **Figure 2-7** EtherTalk data packet format

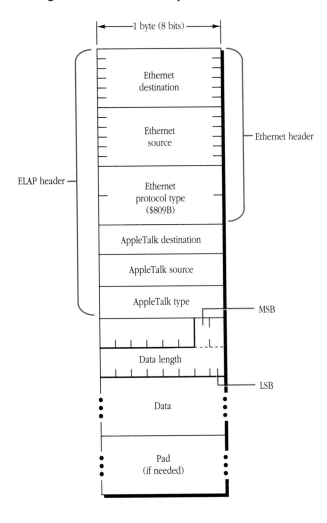

To establish a node's protocol address, EtherTalk's implementation of AARP randomly picks a temporary AppleTalk address at initialization time. AARP then sends probe packets with the temporary address to determine if another node is currently using the address.

When a node with the arbitrarily assigned address receives the probe packet (that is, when its address matches the destination address of the probe packet), it returns a response packet to the node that initiated the probe. AARP then assigns another address to the device and sends out more probe packets. When AARP fails to receive a response to a probe packet, the address in the packet is assigned to the device until it is switched off. A Macintosh computer keeps its latest AppleTalk address in parameter RAM. When the node is switched off and back on, AARP tries that address first.

To send data packets, a transmitting AARP client node requests from AARP the hardware address that corresponds to the protocol address of the receiving node. AARP retrieves this address from the AMT and returns it to its client.

If a requested address is not present in the AMT, AARP sends request packets to all nodes on the network. The node with this protocol address sends a response packet, and AARP updates the AMT. If no response comes after a specific time period, AARP assumes that the node does not exist and returns an error message to the client.

AARP filters all data packets a node receives, verifying that the destination protocol address of the packet is the same as the node's protocol address or the broadcast address. If the addresses do not match, AARP discards the packet.

Ethernet driver

EtherTalk software includes an Ethernet driver, which is software that controls the hardware that transmits and receives packets on the Ethernet network. The Ethernet driver is the interface between the 'atlk' resource and the EtherTalk Interface Card. The driver, named .ENET, resides in the System file.

LANSTAR AppleTalk

LANSTAR AppleTalk is an implementation of the AppleTalk protocols on Northern Telecom's high-speed, twisted-pair local area network, Meridian LANSTAR. Using a star **topology,** the Meridian LANSTAR system offers high transmission speeds to Macintosh II computers connected to a star controller, called the LANSTAR Packet Transport Cabinet. The star controller routes data packets to the appropriate node. Each node connects directly to the star controller independently of other nodes on the network (see *Figure 2-8*).

The star topology of LANSTAR AppleTalk can be expanded easily without disrupting service to other devices on the network. Since each device is isolated, problems at one node do not affect any of the other nodes.

■ **Figure 2-8** LANSTAR AppleTalk network

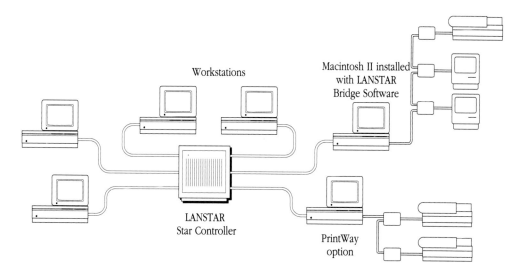

LANSTAR uses two twisted-pair cables (four wires), which may run up to 2000 feet from the central star and may support up to 1344 active nodes with transmission speeds of up to 2.56 Mbps. Within the star controller, data transmission rates reach 40 Mbps.

LANSTAR AppleTalk requires

- a LANSTAR Interface Card for each Macintosh II
- LANSTAR AppleTalk software (Workstation, PrintWay, or Bridge versions) for each Macintosh II
- an installed Meridian LANSTAR network

The LANSTAR AppleTalk Interface Card is a NuBus™ interface card designed for the Macintosh II. It provides the physical connection between the Macintosh II and the Meridian LANSTAR network. For more information, refer to Northern Telecom's *Meridian LANSTAR for the Macintosh II User's Guide.*

By installing optional background bridge software (which actually functions as a router) on a Macintosh II workstation, computers that are not Macintosh II models may be included in the LANSTAR AppleTalk network. These computers form a LocalTalk network, which then connects to the LANSTAR AppleTalk network via the software bridge. The software bridge functions run in the background on the Macintosh II and remain transparent to the user.

LANSTAR AppleTalk software can include the PrintWay option, which allows workstations to print on LaserWriters included in the network. See Chapter 3, "Network Services, Maintenance, and Applications," for more information on printing options.

Connectivity: A review

AppleTalk's protocol architecture supports the inclusion of different link access and physical layer protocols, therefore different media can be used in an AppleTalk network (see *Table 2-1*). LocalTalk is the most economical and easily installed local work group connection, because the necessary transceiver hardware is built into every Macintosh computer and most peripheral devices.

Physical constraints or an organization's needs may dictate that a network use cabling or transceiver types other than those available with LocalTalk. Higher-speed media are available, as well as media that can connect larger work groups over longer distances.

An EtherTalk system using thick or thin Ethernet coaxial cable supports a large number of network devices, offering higher bandwidth over a longer distance than twisted-pair LocalTalk. A LANSTAR AppleTalk system uses twisted-pair cabling in a star configuration, and supports more devices with a faster transmission rate than LocalTalk.

■ **Table 2-1** Media features

	LocalTalk	Thick Ethernet	Thin Ethernet	LANSTAR AppleTalk
Medium	Twisted-pair	Coaxial	Coaxial	Twisted-pair
Link access protocol	LLAP	IEEE 802.3	IEEE 802.3	LLAP
Transmission rate	230.4 Kbps	10 Mbps	10 Mbps	2.56 Mbps
Maximum length	1000 ft.	segment: 1640 ft. network: 8202 ft.	segment: 656 ft. network: 3281 ft.	2000 ft. to star
Distance between nodes	No minimum	8.2 ft. minimum	8.2 ft. minimum	No minimum
Maximum number of nodes	32	segment: 200 network: 1023	segment: 30 network: 1023	1344
Maximum number of active AppleTalk nodes	32	254	254	1344

Chapter 3 **Network Services, Maintenance, and Applications**

THE "WHAT" OF THE NETWORK—the devices and hardware that connect them—is a necessary precondition for enabling users of different types of workstations to share information and resources. Yet it is the "how" of the network—the services it provides as well as the programs, drivers, and protocols—that differentiates between systems and serves both users and developers. The remainder of this book is concerned primarily with the how of AppleTalk.

This chapter consists of four sections, each concerned with a specific area of network use. The sections "Sharing files" and "Printing files" introduce file servers and print servers, discussing their advantages and features. The section "Network troubleshooting" contains information on Inter•Poll™, Apple's software for troubleshooting networks, and is of interest primarily to those administering a network. Network application developers will be most interested in the last section, "Developing network applications," which lists issues to consider when creating shared applications. ■

Sharing files

Within an AppleTalk network system, an AppleShare file server provides a location where a user on the network can store and access common files without disrupting other users' activities (see *Figure 3-1*).

With AppleShare File Server software installed, a Macintosh computer with one or more hard disk drives can become a dedicated file server, that is, a computer used exclusively for storing and sharing information. An AppleShare file server can also be configured as an AppleShare print server, as discussed in the section "Printing files."

Each hard disk attached to an AppleShare file server is called a **volume.** When a user selects a volume, its icon appears on the user's workstation desktop; the volume then functions the same way as any attached disk drive. Apple II and PC users select volumes from the file server by following the appropriate procedures for those computers. Within a volume, files are stored in **folders.** Folders on an AppleShare server volume are analogous to directories on a PC; both are named entities that hold files or other folders or directories. Each folder has an owner who determines which users may access the folder.

■ **Figure 3-1** AppleShare File Server

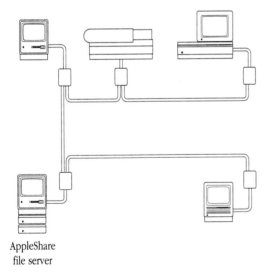

AppleShare
file server

Access privileges control access to information on the file server so the contents of a folder can be kept private, shared by a group of users, or shared by all network users who have access to that volume. Before using the file server, a user is registered, given a password, and placed into one or more groups if appropriate. This user information determines a user's access privileges when he or she tries to access a folder.

Workstations other than Macintosh computers can be configured so that their users may gain full access to an AppleShare file server or print server on an AppleTalk network. Apple IIe computers with an interface card installed and Apple IIGS computers can connect to the network and access the file or print server. PCs connecting to an AppleTalk network require the LocalTalk PC Card and AppleShare PC Workstation Software as detailed in the section "Accessing AppleShare, From a PC."

On an AppleShare file server, user groupings, file organization, file access, and message posting can be controlled by users on the network. Maintenance duties fall to the system administrator, whose role is covered in the section "Administering the AppleShare File Server."

From a Macintosh, a user accesses the file server by opening the Chooser, then logging on and selecting the appropriate volume through a series of windows. The volume's icon appears on the workstation desktop, much like a hard-disk icon. The user can then open and save files and create folders in the same way on a file server volume as on a local disk. Other workstation types also see a server volume as if it were one of their own, directly connected to the workstation.

The log-on process assures security and confidentiality, as users must enter a name and password before accessing protected volumes or folders. Unregistered users may be allowed to log on as guests and gain access to unprotected information.

Access privileges

Macintosh users set, review, and change access privileges for a folder or volume by following the procedures described in this section. Other workstation types follow different but functionally equivalent procedures. These privileges enable users to see folders or files or to make changes. By selecting Get Privileges from the Finder™ File menu, the user can view information for a specific volume or folder (see *Figure 3-2*).

■ **Figure 3-2** Selecting a folder to view access privileges

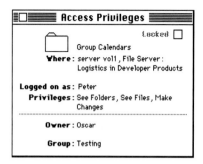

The information in the dialog box includes the volume name, the user's name, the user's privileges, the folder's owner, and the name of the group associated with the folder. If the user is also the owner, the access privileges and settings appear (see *Figure 3-3*). The owner can change the settings, change the group, or transfer ownership to another user. Once ownership of a folder is transferred, only the new owner can change its access privileges.

■ **Figure 3-3** Owner's access privileges

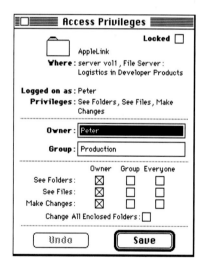

Access privileges to a folder may be granted to any of three user categories: owner, group, and everyone. *Owner* refers to the folder's owner, *group* means the group of users associated with that folder, and *everyone* means every user with access to the server. For a folder, each user category can have any combination of the following access privileges: See Folders, See Files, and Make Changes.

See Folders allows the owner, group, or everyone only to see but not to change the other folders in that folder. See Files allows them to see files in that folder as well as to open and copy any of those files (unless a file is copy-protected), again without changing them. Make Changes allows changes to abe made to that folder's contents.

If the window lists <*any user*> (meaning any registered user) as owner of the folder or volume, any registered user can claim ownership of it. A folder created by a user logged on to the file server as a guest is owned by <any user>.

A folder's owner can prevent accidental changes to the folder by locking it. Users cannot rename, discard, or move locked folders on the volume. Locking a folder, however, does not change the access privileges to it or affect what users can do with the folder's contents.

Special-purpose folders

AppleShare's access privileges lend themselves particularly well to creating special areas for posting messages and dropping off information. These special-purpose areas are simply folders acting as bulletin boards or drop boxes.

A bulletin board is an area where any user can access messages. When creating a bulletin board folder, the owner restricts the Make Changes privileges to himself so no one else can change or post documents (see *Figure 3-4*).

■ **Figure 3-4** Setting up a bulletin board

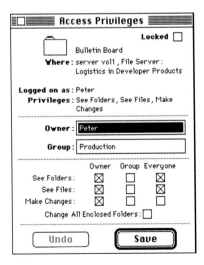

Drop folders are similar to mailslots in an office. They allow users to drop off documents in a specific area but prevent them from seeing what else is there. Such folders are handy when several users each have confidential information to give one user. An owner creates a drop folder by giving all users Make Changes privileges but not See Folders or See Files privileges.

Administering the AppleShare file server

An AppleShare administrator is a person who sets up an AppleShare file server, keeps track of registered users, and maintains the server. The administrator may also set up logical groups of registered users. The main responsibility of the administrator is to keep the server running smoothly.

Installation requirements

Successful integration of an AppleShare file server into an AppleTalk network system requires certain hardware and software, including

■ a Macintosh Plus, Macintosh SE, or Macintosh II computer (which becomes the file server)

■ an Apple Hard Disk 20 (only with a Macintosh Plus), a Hard Disk SC, or compatible hard disk drive

■ an *AppleShare File Server: Server Installer* disk

■ an *AppleShare File Server: Server Administration* disk

The file server is attached to an AppleTalk network in the same manner as other devices. When a Macintosh is configured as an AppleShare file server, it cannot be used as an individual workstation.

Users may gain access to the file server with a Macintosh 512K enhanced, Macintosh Plus, Macintosh SE, or Macintosh II computer using one of two disks:

■ the *AppleShare File Server: Workstation Installer, For use with the Macintosh 512K enhanced only,* or

■ the *AppleShare File Server: Workstation Installer, For use with the Macintosh Plus, SE, and II.*

Apple IIGS and Apple IIe computers and PCs can also be attached to the network and use the file server, if they are set up with the appropriate hardware and software.

Volume requirements

The AppleShare Admin application on the *AppleShare File Server: Server Administration* disk prepares server volumes and creates a **server folder** on each volume, which contains AppleShare-specific files related to the volume, allowing the server software to recognize it as a valid file server volume. The server folder is invisible to users on the network. Users cannot read the contents of the server folder, write to it, or delete it.

Within the server folder is a file called the Parallel Directory Structure (PDS), which has the same hierarchical structure as the **Hierarchical File System (HFS)** catalog. The PDS contains server-specific information for each file and folder in the volume.

Using the administration program, the administrator identifies one server volume as the **startup volume,** which keeps the server application and related files in its server folder. The startup volume's server folder contains:

- the System file and related files
- the startup application called AShare File Srv
- the Parallel Directory Structure
- the Users and Groups file
- optional concurrent applications (described below)

Each file server may have only one startup volume, which must be a valid AppleShare file server volume. A valid volume can be any unlocked and writeable HFS volume. However, the Apple Hard Disk 20 can be used only with a Macintosh Plus set up as a file server.

The AppleCD SC™ can be a valid server volume, but it cannot be used as the startup volume because its contents are read-only. To use a CD-ROM volume, the CD-ROM driver must be installed on the startup volume and the *AppleShare File Server: Server Administration* disk.

Setting up the file server and workstations

After the network has been properly cabled and the administrator has prepared the file server by installing the latest system files and the server software on the startup volume, the administrator runs the AppleShare Admin program on the *AppleShare File Server: Server Administration* disk. At the initial installation, this program requires its user to select the startup volume, name the file server, prepare any additional volumes, and identify the administrator, who will automatically own the server volumes and any unowned folders.

When the computer is restarted, the file server starts itself up automatically. The AppleShare server status window appears on the screen to indicate that the server is available (see *Figure 3-5*). If the administrator selected a concurrent startup application, it also starts, and its windows appear on the server screen instead of the server status window.

■ **Figure 3-5** AppleShare server status window

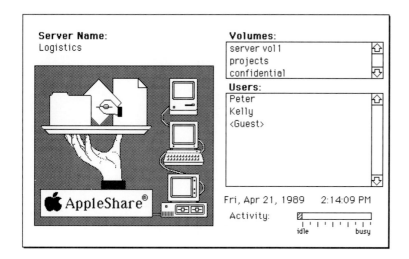

Each workstation on the network needs specific software to access the file server. Running the AppleShare Installer on the appropriate *AppleShare Workstation Installer* disk accomplishes this setup. The AppleShare Installer prompts for the name of the disk on which to install, and displays a message when the process is finished.

Registering users

The AppleShare administrator uses the AppleShare Admin program to add new users and set up user groups. The administrator first enters each user's name and password (see *Figure 3-6*).

Groups may be organized in any fashion: by project, department, or location. The network administrator names the group and selects users for that group. Groups may contain any number of users, and a user can be assigned to up to 16 groups (1 primary group and 15 others). A user's primary group is a convenience feature that assigns a default group name to any folder the user creates.

The Users and Groups file contains all user and group names. The administrator should save this file in a safe place for easy retrieval.

■ **Figure 3-6** Registering users

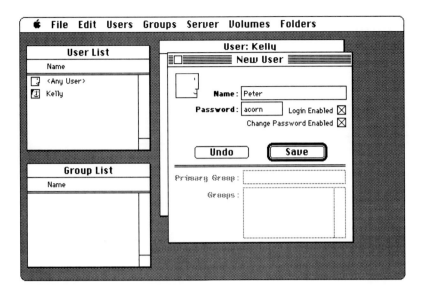

Maintaining the file server

Maintenance duties include backing up file server volumes, keeping records and logs, and producing AppleShare administrative reports. Quite often, the administrator also becomes a resource person for the users.

Accurate records are necessary to see how the server is working and how performance can be improved. These records should include

■ a physical map of the network, with connections, devices, and cable routing clearly marked

■ a list of registered users and passwords

■ a record of Server and Volume Reports

■ a record of AppleShare messages displayed at startup

Some ways to improve performance include running large applications from local hard disks rather than from the server volume and logging off the server when it is not needed.

AppleShare displays messages that can help locate problems. Some messages that appear on the screen at startup and other diagnostic messages are saved in the AppleShare messages file. The messages file can be read from the server status window or the AppleShare Admin program.

Administrative reports provide information about the server and volumes, such as space used, existing files and folders, folder hierarchy and access privileges, and owner, group, and user names. The AppleShare Admin program can be used to create server and volume reports.

All records should be kept in a safe place that is easily accessible to the administrator. Accurate network maps and user listings are crucial for trouble-shooting. Maintaining complete records is also an invaluable aid in the transfer of administrative duties.

Using concurrent applications

Several server applications can be made available to users on the network at the same time the server is available. Such applications are called *concurrent applications,* which may be used one at a time while the file server is active. AppleShare Admin is a concurrent application; network administrators can run this program while users are accessing the file server. AppleShare Print Server software is also a concurrent application. In this case, the print server runs in the *foreground,* meaning its menus and windows appear on the screen and its commands can be used, while the file server runs in the *background,* and its screens cannot be monitored until the print server is shut down.

Accessing AppleShare

An AppleShare file server provides a central storage area and a platform for sharing files for all workstations on the network. Macintosh users simply install the appropriate AppleShare software and log on to the server and use its volumes as if they were hard disks attached directly to their computers. Likewise, Apple II and PC workstations on the network can be configured to access the file server. Apple IIe computers with an Apple II Workstation Card installed and Apple IIGS computers may also connect to an AppleTalk network, thereby gaining access an AppleShare file server. AppleShare PC software and a network interface card such as the LocalTalk PC Card and driver enable PC users to work with an AppleShare file server by means of a menu-based user interface.

From a Macintosh workstation

Once the AppleShare software is installed on a workstation startup disk, that workstation can access a file server. Users access a server from the Chooser, selecting the AppleShare server icon and the appropriate file server from the Chooser window (see *Figure 3-7*). An internet may be subdivided into zones, logical groupings of networks within an internet. In this case the zone must also be selected before choosing the file server.

■ **Figure 3-7** Selecting a file server

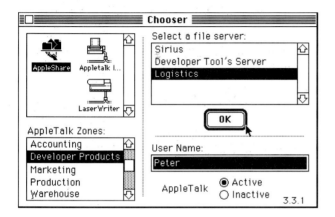

The user then logs on as a registered user or a guest (see *Figure 3-8*), although the network administrator can set up the file server to prevent guests from logging on. Guests have access to unprotected information, although they may not protect information themselves. During the log-on process, the user's password is scrambled to prevent network eavesdroppers from reading it.

■ **Figure 3-8** Logging on to the file server

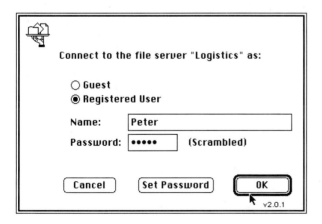

After logging on, the user selects one or more volumes (see *Figure 3-9*), which can be set to open automatically when the workstation restarts. Optionally, the workstation can be set to remember the user's password. If a volume's name is dimmed, it means that the user does not have the right to select it or that it is currently on the user's desktop.

- **Figure 3-9** Selecting a volume

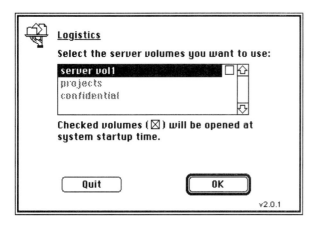

Once a volume is open, the user can store and retrieve information as though it were on a disk attached to the user's workstation. A file server icon appears for each volume (see *Figure 3-10*).

- **Figure 3-10** File server icon

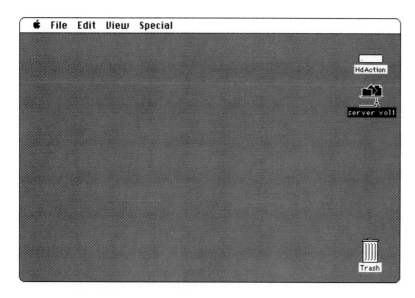

Since the file server is a shared resource, only a limited number of workstations can use it at one time, so those not actively working with it should log off to free it for others. To log off, the user drags the volume icon to the Trash or shuts down the computer.

From an Apple II

Access to an AppleShare file server is not limited to Macintosh computers. Both Apple IIe and Apple IIGS computers can also function as AppleShare workstations, sharing files with other users of AppleShare file servers. Apple IIe computers require the Apple II Workstation Card to connect it to an AppleTalk network. Since the Apple IIGS has LocalTalk hardware built in, it needs no additional hardware.

The Apple II Workstation Card is similar to the LocalTalk hardware built into the Apple IIGS. It contains firmware to control the link between the AppleTalk network and the Apple II. The software that uses the AppleTalk protocols to interact with the server resides on the card. Other AppleShare software is read from the *AppleShare IIe Workstation* disk.

Instead of reading AppleShare software from a disk, both the Apple IIe and the Apple IIGS computers can start up over the network. That is, all the operating system software needed to operate the computer can be read over the network from a specially configured AppleShare file server. Setting up Apple II workstations to start up over the network is the simplest and easiest way to get started. These computers need not have an attached disk drive.

Apple II Installation Requirements

To use the services of an AppleTalk network, an enhanced Apple IIe requires:

- at least 128K of RAM
- an Apple II Workstation Card package, which includes the card, the back panel adapter box and its accessory bag, and the *AppleShare IIe Workstation* disk
- a LocalTalk Connector Kit Din 8

An Apple IIGS requires:

- at least 512K of additional RAM on an Apple IIGS Memory Expansion Card (768K total RAM)
- an AppleShare IIGS Workstation software package, which includes the *AppleShare IIGS Workstation* disk
- a LocalTalk Connector Kit Din 8

With these products, enhanced Apple IIe and Apple IIGS computers can take advantage of many of the services available on AppleTalk networks. Apple II users can use file server volumes just as they use local disk drives and print to LaserWriter and ImageWriter II printers. Additionally, Apple II workstations can start up over the network and run without any attached disk drives. These products, and Apple's Aristotle™ Menu software, are the basis for Apple's solution for networking computers in a classroom.

From a PC

IBM PCs and compatibles can also connect to an AppleTalk network. AppleShare PC software offers MS-DOS compatible workstations access to an AppleShare file server or print server (see *Figure 3-11*). With AppleShare PC software and a LocalTalk PC Card installed, PC users can access file server volumes and printers on an AppleTalk network.

The LocalTalk PC Card contains firmware to control the link between the AppleTalk network and the PC. The LocalTalk PC driver software implements many of the AppleTalk protocols and interacts with the card to send and receive packets.

■ **Figure 3-11** AppleShare PC gives PCs access to an AppleShare file server

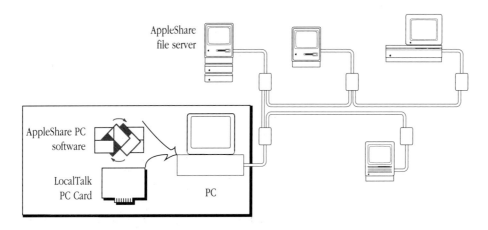

AppleShare PC software consists of four modules (see *Figure 3-12*):

■ The user interface module appears as an AppleTalk desk accessory, through which the PC connects to an AppleShare file server and selects a printer.

■ The MS-DOS Redirector module, which converts all DOS file system requests to Server Message Blocks (SMBs), MS-DOS equivalents of **AppleTalk Filing Protocol (AFP)** calls. (The AppleShare file server uses AFP calls; AFP is discussed in Chapter 4.)

- **Figure 3-12** AppleShare PC file access model

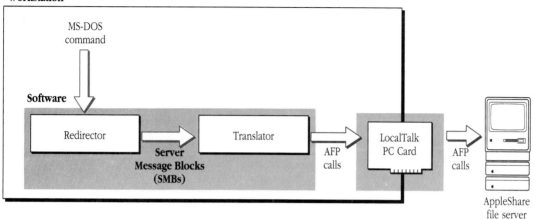

- The Server Message Block-to-AppleTalk Filing Protocol translator module, which converts SMBs to AFP calls. The translator interacts with the LocalTalk PC Card to access the AppleTalk network.
- The installation program module, which installs the AppleShare PC software.

AppleShare PC installation requirements

Before a PC can access a file server, the AppleTalk network must be set up and running. The PC requires:

- the AppleShare PC Installer disk
- at least 384K of RAM
- version 2.0 or greater of the LocalTalk PC Card and driver
- a LocalTalk Connector Kit
- version 3.1 or greater of MS-DOS with SHARE.EXE

AppleShare PC features

AppleShare PC provides a PC user with the same ability as a Macintosh user to access an AppleShare file server, print server, or LaserWriter or ImageWriter II printers. Specifically, a PC user can

- select the zone, server, and server volumes through a menu- and window-based interface

- use server volumes as if they were locally attached disks

- view access privileges for folders on server volumes and set access privileges for folders the user owns

- obtain information about files and folders on the server

Thus AppleShare PC software gives Macintosh and PC workstations a means of sharing documents and storage space. The PC gains the ability to communicate on an AppleTalk network but retains its own user interface because AppleShare PC follows all MS-DOS conventions.

Different workstation types may not generally share applications, since the machines are not object-code compatible. However, all files are potentially visible to all machines on the network. The files can be interchanged if the application software is capable of interpreting data structured in other file formats, and applications that do this are available. (Alternatively, Apple File Exchange may be used to translate files between different workstation formats.)

Printing files

Printing on a network can be accomplished with several hardware and software configurations. AppleTalk systems support both direct printing and printing with a spooler. AppleTalk also supports a remote printing facility, the Asynchronous LaserWriter driver. LANSTAR AppleTalk's PrintWay option gives a workstation in a LANSTAR AppleTalk network access to the LaserWriter.

The printer referred to in this section is the Apple LaserWriter, but the concepts here also apply to other printers that can be used within an AppleTalk network. For more information refer to the Apple publications *Print Spooling in an AppleTalk Network* and *Inside AppleTalk*.

Direct printing

Direct printing occurs when a workstation sends a print job directly to the printer (see *Figure 3-13*). This renders the workstation initiating the print command unavailable for other purposes until the printer finishes the print job.

■ **Figure 3-13** Configuration for direct printing

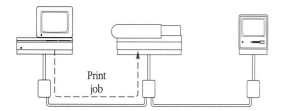

Print
job

When a user issues a command to print a document, the application begins a series of AppleTalk calls via the Print Manager, which attempts to establish a connection with the printer. The calls first initiate the **Name Binding Protocol (NBP)** name-lookup operation to find the AppleTalk address of the currently selected printer. Then the **Printer Access Protocol (PAP)** tries to open a connection with the printer.

Once the connection is established, the workstation and the printer interact over the PAP connection. PAP uses the **AppleTalk Transaction Protocol (ATP)** to send the print files to the printer (see *Figure 3-14*). For more information on NBP, PAP, and ATP, see Chapter 4, "AppleTalk Protocols," and *Inside AppleTalk*.

■ **Figure 3-14** Protocols applied in direct printing

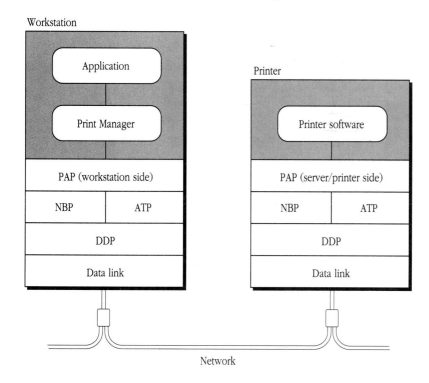

If the printer is busy, the workstation keeps trying to open the connection until the printer finishes the current job. During this time, the workstation cannot be used for any other work. The length of time the workstation is unavailable depends on the printer's speed, the size and type (such as text or graphics) of the print file, and the number of other workstations contending for use of the printer.

Printing with an AppleShare print server

Print spooler software handles the interaction between workstations and the printer, allowing the workstations that send print jobs to be freed for other uses. Two types of spoolers can be used with AppleTalk: a background spooler and a spooler/server.

Background spooler software is loaded into a workstation, which may then send a print job to the user's local disk allowing the workstation to perform other tasks. The job remains on the disk and the spooler runs in the background until the printer becomes available. The workstation must remain connected to the network until the job is processed. The MultiFinder™ PrintMonitor application is one such background spooler.

A **spooler/server** is a dedicated computer distinct from the workstation and printer. It acts as an intermediary between the workstation and the printer (see *Figure 3-15*). When working with a spooler/server, the workstation produces a print file and sends it to the spooler/server. The spooler/server then takes charge of getting the job processed by the printer.

An AppleShare print server is a spooler/server that can run by itself as a dedicated machine, or it can run as a concurrent application with an AppleShare file server.

■ **Figure 3-15** Configuration for printing with a spooler/server

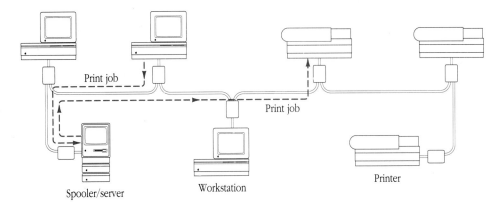

Print job

Print job

Spooler/server

Workstation

Printer

After receiving the print file, the spooler/server terminates its connection with the workstation. The workstation can then perform other tasks or be switched off.

A spooler/server works by setting itself up as a surrogate printer. This means that when the workstation tries to print, the spooler/server appears indistinguishable from a printer to the workstation.

The spooler/server responds to a PAP connection request from a workstation exactly the way a printer would (see *Figure 3-16*). Once the connection is established, the spooler then emulates the workstation's interaction with a printer while storing the files to be printed in its internal buffer. The spooler/server then takes over the task of waiting for the printer to process the job.

LaserWriters and other printers accept only one job, or connection, at a time. Spooler/servers can accept several connections at a time and then send them to the printer in the order received or another predetermined order, thereby minimizing the contention problems that occur when the users of several workstations try to print directly at the same time.

■ **Figure 3-16** Protocols applied in printing with a spooler/server

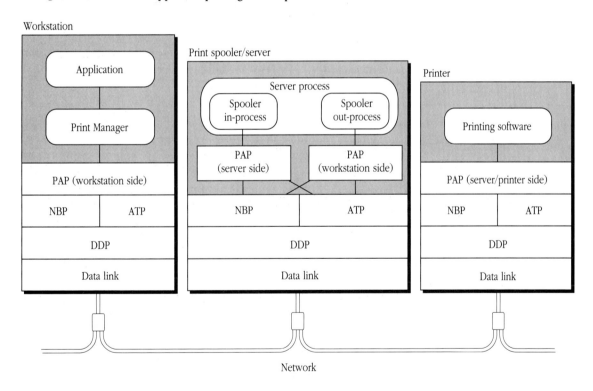

Developers can modify the print spooling architecture in order to spool to printers directly plugged into the spooler/server or to printers that communicate through a protocol other than PAP (see *Figure 3-17*). In these cases, the spooler accepts the print files from the workstation in the same manner but modifies the way it sends the print files to meet the specific needs of the different printer.

■ **Figure 3-17** Protocols applied in alternative spooling environments

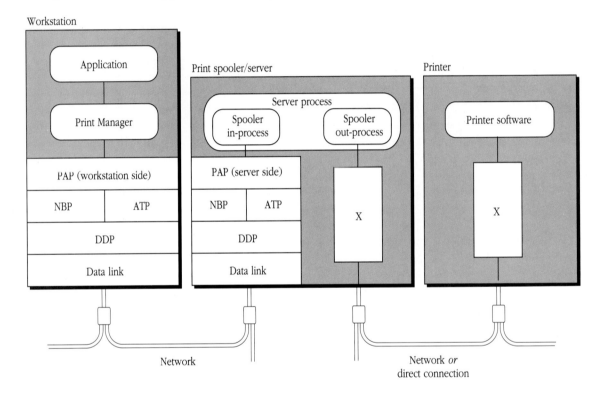

Printing from a PC

The AppleTalk PC printer driver enables a PC to print to LaserWriter, ImageWriter II, and ImageWriter LQ printers from within an application. The *AppleShare PC User's Guide* contains a complete description of the AppleShare PC software capabilities and the AppleTalk PC driver. For information on the LocalTalk Card and driver and printing from a PC, see the *LocalTalk PC Card Owner's Guide*.

Print server functions

The primary role of a print spooler is to free workstations during the printing process. The AppleTalk protocol architecture for print spooling is flexible enough to support such spooler services as:

- printer access control
- user authentication
- direct pass-through
- queue management

Because the spooler/server lies functionally between workstation and printer, it can easily control printer access. This setup also provides an ideal location for user authentication as well as for gathering statistics about printer use.

User authentication can occur just after the workstation opens a PAP connection to the spooler/server or printer. The devices can exchange a series of messages known as the user-authentication dialog. The exact mechanism for authentication depends on the printer.

To restrict direct access to a printer, the spooler/server renames the printer so that other network devices cannot find it. The spooler/server then names itself as a printer. As a result, when workstations search for the printer, they find the spooler/server instead.

Developers may design the spooler/server so that workstations can send print jobs directly to the printer, passing through the spooler. With this direct pass-through method, the spooler does not spool files for printing but simply relays messages between the workstation and printer.

Queue management functions may be incorporated into the spooler/server design. Some useful functions include the ability to rearrange the order of print jobs, move print jobs from one spooler queue to another, and remove print jobs.

The Asynchronous LaserWriter driver

The Asynchronous LaserWriter driver provides remote printing ability, meaning the workstation and printer are not connected directly to the same network. Printing is done via asynchronous connection methods, which follow connect protocols written with the Asynchronous Connection Language (ACL). This system requires:

- Macintosh workstations
- an Apple LaserWriter or LaserWriter Plus

- a connection between the Macintosh and LaserWriter, such as an asynchronous modem

- the *Asynchronous LaserWriter Driver* disk

A typical system might connect Macintosh computers to the telephone network with Apple Personal Modems. The LaserWriter could be connected to the telephone network with a modem capable of automatic answering.

With this configuration, dial-up access is available to an unlimited number of users. If a data line or modem is already in place, there are usually no additional cable costs required to access the LaserWriter.

The Asynchronous Connection Language produces scripts that the Asynchronous LaserWriter driver interprets to connect a Macintosh to a LaserWriter using Hayes-compatible modems. Using ACL, the scripts can be edited to facilitate connection using some other modem, telecommunications device, PBX, or public data network.

The ACL file handles several tasks. It

- recognizes possible error conditions

- checks that the driver is working and connected to the Macintosh

- tells the driver to dial the network

- establishes the connection with the LaserWriter

- backs out of a connection, if necessary

Once the Macintosh workstation connects successfully, the Asynchronous LaserWriter driver takes over the printing process.

ACL is analogous to Apple's AppleLink® CCL facility, using a similar command interpreter and script language. For ACL syntax and command descriptions, refer to the *Asynchronous LaserWriter Driver Developer's Guide*.

Meridian SL-1 Laser Printer software

Meridian SL-1 Laser Printer software is an example of an Asynchronous LaserWriter driver; it is tailored to Northern Telecom's Meridian SL-1 PBX. With this software installed, the Macintosh and LaserWriter can communicate through the office PBX.

This system can be set up in several configurations, via the standard data connection method for the Meridian SL-1, via an asynchronous modem, or over the public switched telephone network using modems that support the "AT" style modem command set.

For complete information on this software, refer to the *Meridian SL-1 Laser Printer User's Guide* from Northern Telecom, Inc.

PrintWay option in LANSTAR AppleTalk

LANSTAR AppleTalk's PrintWay option provides local printing capabilities for Macintosh II workstations on Meridian's LANSTAR network. A Macintosh II workstation must have LANSTAR AppleTalk's PrintWay option installed and must be connected to a LaserWriter via a standard LocalTalk connection (see *Figure 3-18*).

The three standard configurations are:

■ PrintWay installed on a Macintosh II

■ PrintWay installed on a Macintosh II set up as an AppleShare file server

■ PrintWay installed on a Macintosh II set up as an AppleShare file server and an AppleShare print server

A Macintosh II with PrintWay installed functions as a router and must be turned on before any workstations can access the printer. The Macintosh II remains available as a workstation, but its performance may be impaired when other workstations are printing.

A Macintosh II that runs as an AppleShare file server or an AppleShare print server can concurrently run PrintWay software.

Northern Telecom's *Meridian LANSTAR for the Macintosh II User's Guide* contains more information on the LANSTAR AppleTalk environment.

■ **Figure 3-18** PrintWay option in LANSTAR AppleTalk

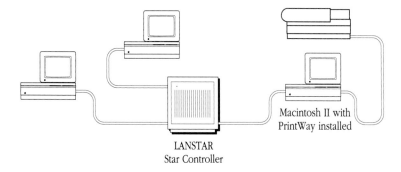

LANSTAR
Star Controller

Macintosh II with
PrintWay installed

Network troubleshooting (Inter•Poll)

Careful planning, monitoring, and maintenance are essential if users are to realize the potential of a network. Network troubleshooting involves determining how the system should work and keeping it working. Apple's Inter•Poll Network Administrator's Utility software tool helps network administrators plan the optimum network layout, monitor network performance, and analyze problems should they arise. Inter•Poll searches for and reports on the active devices in an AppleTalk network, helping network administrators find trouble spots before users experience problems.

Inter•Poll features

Inter•Poll helps isolate network problem areas. The AppleTalk system administrator's workstation should have Inter•Poll installed, since this person is generally responsible for maintaining the network. However, Inter•Poll can be run from any Macintosh (Plus or later models) on the internet.

Inter•Poll can be used to

- display listings of zones, connected networks, and active network devices

- verify the connection status of any part of a network or internet

- test the integrity and response of the network path to a specific device

- localize possible sources of trouble and receive troubleshooting guidelines

- query active workstations in an AppleTalk internet for a report of current system software versions

Inter•Poll also includes a Network Map file, an easy-to-use MacDraw® file that allows administrators to create network maps showing the floor plan, network cabling layout, and the location of each network device (see *Figure 3-19*). The resulting on-line network map encourages the administrator to record changes, since editing the screen is a simple process. A current printed map should always be on hand for troubleshooting, because access to the printer may be difficult or impossible when the network is down.

Optimally, network maintenance and checks should be performed frequently enough to discover problems before they cause trouble for users. The frequency of checks will depend on the size of the network and how much it is used. These checks should encompass the entire network.

■ **Figure 3-19** Network map

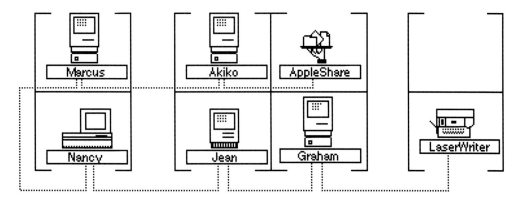

Inter•Poll's troubleshooting strategy is to perform a sequential series of tasks designed to isolate the location of a problem. It begins with a zone and device listing and proceeds to local testing at the device or network level.

Inter•Poll first checks zones, networks, and devices to determine which are present on the internet. Optionally, individual devices can then be checked to assure network integrity by testing for data loss and network path changes resulting from router malfunctions.

Inter•Poll windows

Inter•Poll's features are accessible through a series of menus and windows that help locate and track nodes, test network regions, and check response time.

Network Search window

The Network Search window appears each time Inter•Poll is started (see *Figure 3-20*). Using this window, the administrator can search specific zones by selecting the zone and starting the search. Searches can be made for a set time period and can follow a sorting order chosen by the administrator (by network number, device name, node number, socket number, device type, or zone). The window can also list all devices, or devices that match a given network number, device type, or device name. Some non-Apple devices do not register a name on an AppleTalk network. Such unnamed devices may also be included in network searches.

■ **Figure 3-20** Network Search window

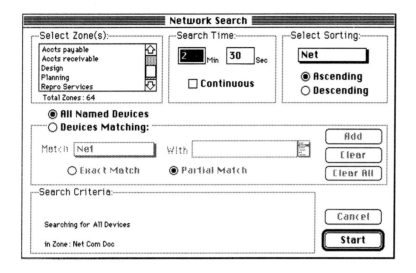

Device List window

Once the network search begins, the Device List window appears, showing the results of the network search in columns that can be individually resized or removed from the display (see *Figure 3-21*). The Device List window displays the results of the network search in columns that can be formatted interactively. The Stop button terminates the search at any time. The resulting list can then be printed or saved as a tab-delimited text file.

■ **Figure 3-21** Device List window

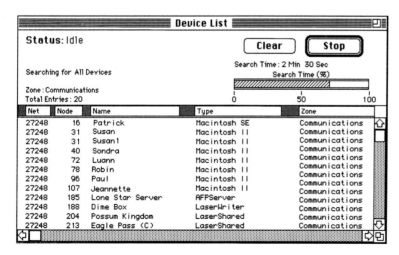

Test Device window

The Test Device window initiates loopback tests, which check connection path integrity and response time between the Inter•Poll workstation and a targeted device (see *Figure 3-22*). By sending test packets to a sequence of devices along a network, the administrator can determine the origin of a transmission problem. Tests may be made by sending echo, printer, or system information packets across the network and/or internet and observing the response network nodes make to the packets.

Echo packets test other workstations and servers. The information returned includes the distance travelled by the packets (in **hops,** that is the number of internet routers they have crossed), time delay (in seconds), and the number of packets sent, received, and lost.

LaserWriters, ImageWriter II printers with the AppleTalk Option, and other devices that use the PAP protocol are tested with printer packets. These tests return distance, time, and number of packets, along with the printer status.

System information packets query Macintosh nodes for current system software versions. Numbers are returned for the System, Finder, LaserWriter driver, Responder, AppleTalk, and AppleShare versions of the targeted node. (Responder is a program installed on a Macintosh workstation that enables Inter•Poll to recognize the node and acquire identifying data when searching the network.)

■ **Figure 3-22** Test Device window

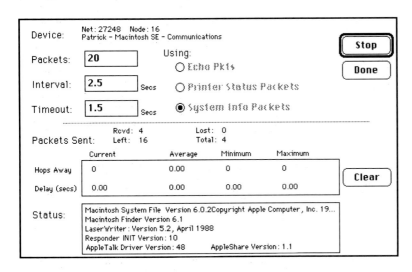

Developing network applications

An AppleShare file server makes it possible to share applications and data by providing a common location for file storage. Several workstations can interact with a file server to read and write the same file, either one at a time or concurrently.

Applications running in workstations access files on an AppleShare server in the same way that they access files on a local disk, by making calls to their **native file system.** If a particular file system call refers to a file that resides on a file server, then the call is routed through a file system translator that converts it into an AppleTalk Filing Protocol (AFP) request. This request is sent to the file server, which services the request and returns a reply to the workstation.

AFP calls are the means by which the file server and a workstation communicate. Since this interaction with the server occurs at a level below the file system, it allows users transparent access to the server volumes and files. For more details on AFP, see Chapter 4 or *Inside AppleTalk.*

The AppleShare File Server environment encourages the development of applications that can be shared. Special considerations are necessary for file management when applications are to be shared across a network, particularly when the applications allow multi-user and multilaunch capabilities.

Application programs developed specifically for network use are categorized by file sharing modes and application launching characteristics (see *Figure 3-23*). Multi-user applications let two or more users make changes to the same file concurrently. Multilaunch applications allow two or more users to open and work simultaneously with one copy of an application.

Applications designed specifically for use on networks should be able to handle simultaneous users, and any associated copyrights should consider that many users may access one copy of the application. Applications not designed for use on shared volumes can be run on an AppleShare file server if certain preconditions are met:

- The application's copyright statement indicates that multiple user access is permissible.

- For an application that creates temporary files, the application resides in a folder for which the users have the privileges See Files and Make Changes. (Applications may put temporary files in the workstation startup disk's System Folder.)

- The documents associated with each application are kept in folders that are private to a single user.

- Applications must use the system files on the workstation's startup disk, because no usable System file or Finder appears in any folder on a server volume.

The Apple publication *Software Applications in a Shared Environment* details these considerations and also contains information on making applications suitable for network use.

■ **Figure 3-23** Network application categories

		File sharing mode	
		Single-user	Multi-user
Application launching characteristics	Single-launch	☐ one user per application	☐ one user per application
		☐ only one user at a time can modify a file	☐ two or more users at a time can modify a file
	Multi-launch	☐ two or more users per application	☐ two or more users per application
		☐ only one user at a time can modify a file	☐ two or more users at a time can modify a file

Networking Services, Maintenance, and Applications: A review

File servers offer a central storage area and a platform for sharing on the network, where all users can store and retrieve files. This enhances productivity to network users by providing easy access to documents, applications, and data files. File service works transparently; each user accesses the file server as if it were a local disk.

A network also allows users to share expensive peripheral devices, such as laser printers. To handle shared printer traffic, a print spooler can temporarily store print jobs and send them to the printer in a predetermined order, freeing the workstations that sent the jobs to perform other tasks. Thus the user saves time normally required for processing the print job and waiting for the printer.

As a network grows, it becomes more difficult to manage. Network management and diagnostic tools and troubleshooting aids such as Apple's Inter•Poll software are essential for maintaining the system's efficiency, monitoring network functions, and diagnosing and repairing problems.

Application developers must look at the special requirements of applications that run in a shared environment. These requirements depend on whether or not the application allows one or more users simultaneously to launch it or to use it to make changes to shared files.

Part II details the way the AppleTalk network system protocols function to allow nodes to communicate with each other and to provide the services discussed in Chapter 3.

Part II AppleTalk Protocols and Their Application

Chapter 4 **AppleTalk Protocols**

THE SECOND HALF OF *AppleTalk Network System Overview* is aimed primarily at developers and details the AppleTalk protocols and drivers. The AppleTalk protocols provide a broad range of network communication features, from basic connectivity to peer-to-peer reliable data streams and beyond. This chapter discusses the functions offered by each of the AppleTalk protocols. Developers may use these protocols or build additional protocols to implement other features. ■

Underlying all use of the AppleTalk network system is a specific set of rules, or protocols, that govern communications. The AppleTalk protocol architecture is divided into layers of protocols, each protocol providing different services needed to send or receive information over the network. The protocols guide information from the cabling or connection system to the user application and vice versa (see *Figure 4-1*).

■ **Figure 4-1** AppleTalk protocol architecture

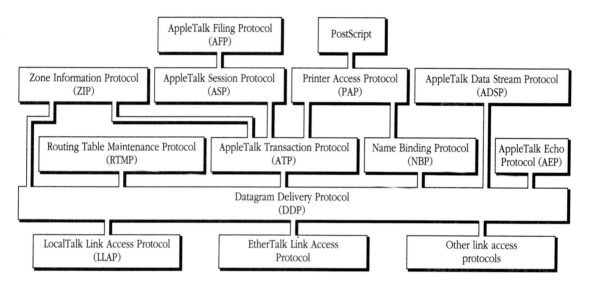

While Apple Computer, Inc., recommends using these protocols, communication via the AppleTalk system is not dependent on their exclusive use. Since the protocols are layered, each controlling a distinct function, developers can substitute alternative protocols. Indeed, the AppleTalk protocol architecture encourages developers to add special features and functions for their particular applications.

User information moves up or down through the AppleTalk protocols by means of a process called **data encapsulation/decapsulation.** As a unit of information moves down through the protocols before transmission, each protocol encapsulates the information with its own header and trailer, as required. When information moves up through the protocols after reception, each protocol strips off its specific header or trailer, decapsulating the data, then interprets the header or trailer information and passes it up to the protocol at the next higher layer.

What are the AppleTalk protocols?

The remainder of this chapter, intended primarily to provide developers a thorough understanding of the AppleTalk protocols, details the protocol layers and core protocols. The AppleTalk protocols reside in the following levels:

- Physical and data link—LocalTalk Link Access Protocol (LLAP), AppleTalk Address Resolution Protocol (AARP)

- End-to-end data flow—Datagram Delivery Protocol (DDP), Routing Table Maintenance Protocol (RTMP), AppleTalk Echo Protocol (AEP)

- Named entities—Name Binding Protocol (NBP), Zone Information Protocol (ZIP)

- Reliable data delivery—AppleTalk Transaction Protocol (ATP), Printer Access Protocol (PAP), AppleTalk Session Protocol (ASP), AppleTalk Data Stream Protocol (ADSP)

- End-user services—AppleTalk Filing Protocol (AFP), PostScript, Print Spooling

Physical layer

Cables such as LocalTalk cable and connector hardware form the AppleTalk physical layer (see *Figure 4-2)*. The physical layer's hardware has the capabilities to:

- encode and decode bits

- synchronize transmissions

- transmit and receive signals

- perform contention resolution (when applicable)

■ **Figure 4-2** Physical layer

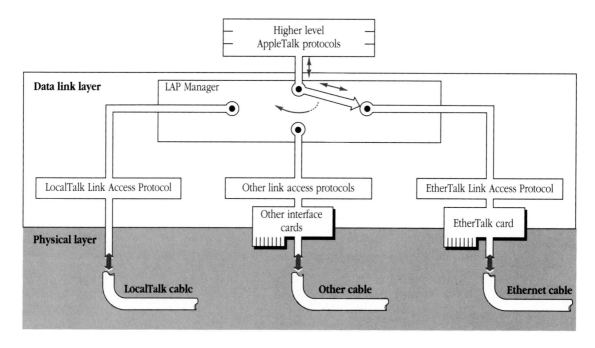

Data links

The data link protocols, which lie between the physical layer and the end-to-end data flow protocols, handle the delivery of information between nodes on a local area network (see *Figure 4-3*). The AppleTalk protocol architecture currently includes three data link layer protocols:

■ LocalTalk Link Access Protocol (LLAP)

■ AppleTalk Address Resolution Protocol (AARP)

■ EtherTalk Link Access Protocol (ELAP)

As in all layers of the AppleTalk protocol architecture, alternative protocols are supported as well. The EtherTalk Link Access Protocol is used with Ethernet media. For information on ELAP, see *EtherTalk and Alternate AppleTalk Connections Reference.*

If the physical medium is LocalTalk, all nodes on the network must use the LocalTalk Link Access Protocol. LLAP delivers information to nodes on a single network. To do this, LLAP

■ mediates access to the link for transmission and reception of data

■ provides a dynamic node addressing mechanism

■ transmits packets between nodes connected to a single AppleTalk network

The link is the path along which information is transmitted, such as the cables and connector modules.

The AppleTalk Address Resolution Protocol provides a mapping service between any two sets of addresses. For example, given a node's Ethernet hardware address, AARP can determine the node's AppleTalk protocol address.

The LAP Manager standardizes interactions between the higher-level AppleTalk protocols and the data link protocols currently being used. With these interactions standardized, the higher-level protocols do not need to account for the differences in the current link access layer characteristics. The LAP manager resides *between* the data link protocols and the remaining higher level protocols.

■ **Figure 4-3** Data link layer

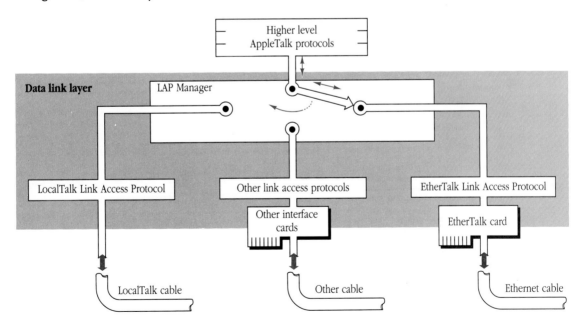

End-to-end data flow

The end-to-end data flow protocols facilitate transmission of data across an internet. Specifically, these protocols allow data delivery across an AppleTalk internet and also provide an echo mechanism. AppleTalk end-to-end data flow protocols are:

- the Datagram Delivery Protocol (DDP)
- the Routing Table Maintenance Protocol (RTMP)
- the AppleTalk Echo Protocol (AEP)

While LLAP delivers information within a single AppleTalk network, the Datagram Delivery Protocol extends information delivery over an AppleTalk internet. DDP also introduces the concept of a **socket,** which is a logical addressable entity within a node. The packets of information exchanged between sockets are called **datagrams;** an individual socket is the source and destination of datagrams.

The **Routing Table Maintenance Protocol (RTMP)** provides the logic required to route datagrams through **router ports** toward destination networks. This protocol allows routers to dynamically discover routes to the different AppleTalk networks in an internet. Other nonrouter nodes use a part of RTMP, the RTMP Stub, to determine the number of the network to which they are connected as well as the addresses of routers on their network.

The **AppleTalk Echo Protocol (AEP)** allows a node to send a datagram to another node and to receive a copy, or an echo, of the datagram. Echoing confirms the existence of a particular node and is useful for measuring round-trip delays. AEP allows any node to send a datagram to any other node on an AppleTalk internet and receive an echoed copy in return.

Named entities

Certain AppleTalk protocols handle naming of network devices. In the AppleTalk network system, these protocols offer name binding and zone information services. The naming protocols are:

- the Name Binding Protocol (NBP)
- the Zone Information Protocol (ZIP)

The Name Binding Protocol enables users to give names to network devices. NBP does this by providing and maintaining translation tables that identify these character string names with their corresponding internet socket addresses.

A zone is a grouping of networks in an internet. The **Zone Information Protocol (ZIP)** maintains an internet-wide map of zone-to-network names. NBP uses the ZIP internet mapping to determine which networks belong to a given zone.

Reliable data delivery

The data delivery protocols guarantee the delivery of data, improving on the best-effort delivery service provided by end-to-end data flow protocols. The set of data delivery protocols is divided into two groups: transaction-based and data stream. Transaction-based protocols are based on a request-response model common in workstation-server interaction. Data stream protocols provide a bidirectional reliable flow of data between two communicating entities.

The reliable data delivery protocols are:

- the AppleTalk Transaction Protocol (ATP)
- the Printer Access Protocol (PAP)
- the AppleTalk Session Protocol (ASP)
- the AppleTalk Data Stream Protocol (ADSP)

An AppleTalk **transaction** takes place when a client of one socket sends to another socket a request to which some response is expected. (Generally, the second socket returns a status report or results of the operation requested.) The AppleTalk Transaction Protocol manages this transaction in a way that binds together the request and response to ensure their reliable exchange.

The Printer Access Protocol creates a connection-oriented transaction service for sending print requests to an Apple LaserWriter and other printing devices.

While ATP manages a transaction reliably, the **AppleTalk Session Protocol (ASP)** maintains a sequence of transactions (requests and responses) over a session. ASP opens, maintains, and closes sessions, and sequences requests.

The **AppleTalk Data Stream Protocol (ADSP)** provides reliable, full-duplex, byte-stream service between any two sockets on an AppleTalk internet. Over its connections, ADSP delivers data in sequence, without duplication.

End-user services

End-user services build upon the functions provided by the highest layer protocols. These include:

- the AppleTalk Filing Protocol (AFP)
- PostScript

Built on ASP, the AppleTalk Filing Protocol allows users to share data files and applications that reside on a shared resource (a file server).

PostScript offers a resolution-independent standard method of describing graphic and textual data. Developed by Adobe Systems, PostScript is a programming language understood by the Apple LaserWriter and other graphic devices. For details, see *Print Spooling in an AppleTalk Network* (published by Apple Computer) and the *PostScript Language Reference Manual* (published by Addison-Wesley).

The remainder of this chapter introduces the protocols, discussing their features and how the protocols work with each other. For complete technical information on the protocols, refer to *Inside AppleTalk*.

LocalTalk Link Access Protocol (LLAP)

The LocalTalk Link Access Protocol allows network devices to share LocalTalk and other communication media and is used for sending information over the medium within a single network (see *Figure 4-4*).

■ **Figure 4-4** LocalTalk Link Access Protocol (LLAP)

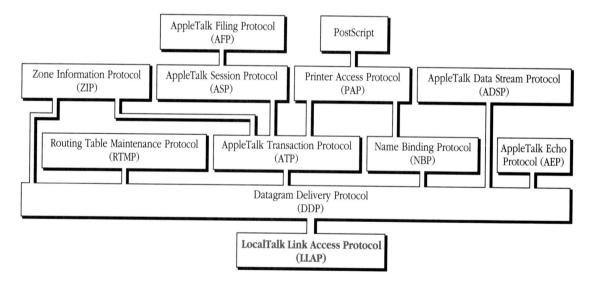

As it transmits data on the bus, LLAP is charged with three tasks:

- providing link access management
- providing a way to address nodes
- performing packet transmission and reception

Link access management

One of LLAP's responsibilities is to manage access to the link. It does this by using **Carrier Sense Multiple Access with Collision Avoidance (CSMA/CA).**

All nodes on a network compete for access to the link. Without a way of controlling admission, data could not be communicated in a uniform, equal, error-free manner. Proper link access management provides fair access for all nodes. CSMA/CA serves as LLAP's tool for ensuring this access.

As its name implies, CSMA/CA performs carrier sense (checks the line for ongoing transmissions before attempting to send a packet), allows multiple access (sharing of the link by more than one node), and provides collision avoidance (minimizing the number of times two or more nodes attempt to transmit packets simultaneously). It performs the latter service by requiring all nodes to wait before transmitting for a set amount of time plus an additional random period based on the current traffic load.

Node addressing

Node addressing is a means of identifying each node on the link. LLAP uses a technique called dynamic node ID assignment, by which a node picks its node number whenever it starts up.

Dynamic node ID assignment

The **node IDs** themselves are assigned dynamically, meaning that a node does not receive a fixed, unique address. Instead, a node assigns itself a number upon starting up. Dynamic node ID assignment offers two advantages over fixed assignment. First, a node doesn't need any additional hardware to define its address. Second, it is unnecessary to administer the assignment of node IDs to different vendors.

Upon starting up, a node randomly assigns itself an ID. It then tests this ID to determine if another node is already using it (see *Figure 4-5*) by sending out an enquiry **control packet,** which in effect checks each node to find out whether it is using the ID. If the ID is not in use, the node retains it. If it is in use, the node already using the ID responds with an acknowledge control packet. When it receives this packet, the new node discards the number, assigns itself a new one, and then tests it. This process continues until the node has a valid unused ID.

■ **Figure 4-5** Under dynamic node ID assignment, a new node tests its randomly assigned ID

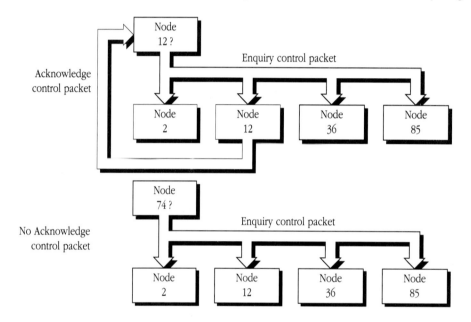

Node identifier numbers

LLAP identifies each node with an 8-bit node identifier number (the node ID, for short). An individual node's ID is its address on the link. Since the IDs are 8 bits, LLAP can dynamically assign up to 256 IDs, 254 of which can be used as addresses (see *Table 4-1*). Node ID 0 is not allowed, and node ID 255 is reserved for a broadcast node ID.

Dividing the ID assignments between the user and server nodes minimizes the negative impact of a node acquiring another node's ID when the latter is busy and cannot respond to the enquiry control packets. This can happen when a node is engaged in a device-intensive operation such as accessing a disk. Excluding user node IDs from the server node ID range eliminates the possibility that a user node will conflict with a server node, a situation that would disrupt service for all users trying to communicate with that user or the server.

■ **Table 4-1** Node ID assignments

Node ID range	Assignment
0	not allowed (unknown)
1–127	user node IDs
128–254	server node IDs
255	broadcast to all nodes on the link

Packet transmission

For the purpose of transmitting information, LLAP distinguishes between two kinds of packets and, consequently, two kinds of transmissions. A **directed packet** is sent to a single node and hence is transmitted via a **directed transmission.** Similarly, a **broadcast packet** goes to all nodes via a **broadcast transmission.**

Data transmission occurs via a dialog between nodes. Prior to this dialog, the sending node determines that the link is clear for the interdialog gap (IDG) of 400 microseconds, plus a random wait period. The individual packets of a given dialog are separated by an interframe gap (IFG) of at most 200 microseconds.

Directed transmissions

Directed transmissions occur according to the following five steps (see *Figure 4-6*):

1. The source node checks the link until it has been idle for one IDG (at least 400 microseconds).
2. The source node then waits for an additional random period.
3. The source node sends a request-to-send (lapRTS) packet to the destination node.
4. The destination node responds with a clear-to-send (lapCTS) packet.
5. The source node transmits a data packet to the destination node.

Steps 3 and 4 (sending the lapRTS and lapCTS packets) have the effect of reserving the communication line. When the source node receives the lapCTS packet, it assumes that all other potential transmitting nodes have heard the lapRTS-lapCTS exchange and will not try to transmit. If a collision occurs during the lapRTS-lapCTS exchange, the source node will not receive the lapCTS packet and will go back to step 1 and begin the process again.

- **Figure 4-6** LapRTS–lapCTS exchange during a directed data transmission

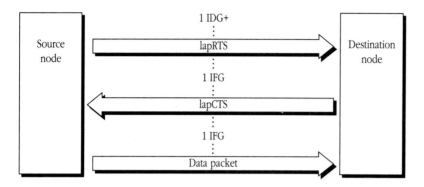

The destination node must send the lapCTS packet within one IFG. Otherwise, the source node assumes that a transmission error has occurred and returns to step 1. The source node will attempt up to 32 retransmissions before reporting failure to the client. The random wait during step 2 minimizes collisions by spreading out transmitters waiting for the line.

Broadcast transmissions

Broadcast transmissions, which go to all nodes on the link, have the destination node ID 255 (address $FF). A collision can occur during a broadcast transmission only in the unlikely event of another node simultaneously attempting a broadcast. Broadcast transmissions occur according to the following five steps:

1. The source node checks the link until it has been idle for one IDG (at least 400 microseconds).
2. The source node then waits for an additional random period.
3. The source node sends a request to send (lapRTS) packet with the broadcast address $FF.
4. The source node checks the line for one IFG (maximum 200 microseconds).
5. The source node broadcasts the transmission.

The lapRTS notifies other potential transmitters of its intent to use the link, causing them to defer their attempt to use the link.

If the source node detects activity during step 4, it returns to step 1 to try again. The source node will attempt up to 32 retransmissions before reporting failure to the client.

Packet reception

A node receives a packet if

- the packet's destination address is the same as the node's (or is the broadcast address)
- the receiving node verifies the packet's frame check sequence (FCS)

A packet's FCS is part of the packet trailer used to detect packets received with errors. The FCS is computed dynamically as a function of a packet's contents. (For complete details on FCS, refer to *Inside AppleTalk*.) The receiving node rejects any bad packets, which result from one of several error conditions, such as a packet that is too large or a packet of the wrong type. LLAP handles these problems directly, without referring them to a higher-level protocol.

AppleTalk Address Resolution Protocol (AARP)

The AppleTalk Address Resolution Protocol resides between the link access protocol and the LAP Manager (see *Figure 4-7*).

- **Figure 4-7** AppleTalk Address Resolution Protocol (AARP)

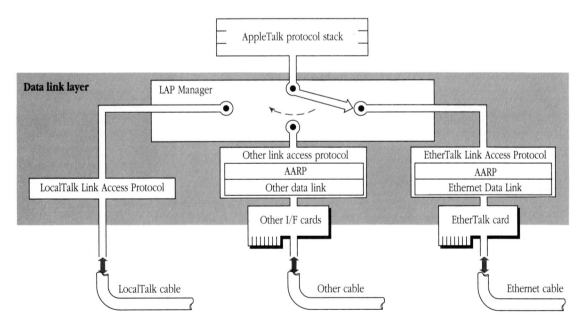

AARP performs three basic functions. It

■ initially determines the unique protocol address of an AppleTalk node for a given protocol set (such as the AppleTalk protocols)

■ maps between two address sets

■ filters packets within a given protocol set

Within a node, AARP maintains an Address Mapping Table (AMT) for a given protocol set. In the case of EtherTalk, the AMT contains a list of AppleTalk protocol addresses and their corresponding Ethernet hardware addresses. (For more information about AMTs, see the section "Maintaining the Address Mapping Table.")

AARP maps between *any* two sets of addresses, but this section discusses primarily EtherTalk's implementation of AARP, in which AARP maps Ethernet hardware addresses to AppleTalk protocol addresses. As such, most examples in the section show the hardware address-to-protocol address mapping scheme, although the examples and discussions apply as well for any protocol-to-protocol mapping.

A node's protocol address is unique, distinct from that of any other node attached to the network. Given a protocol address for a node's protocol set, AARP returns a corresponding hardware address for that node (or an error, if no node has such a protocol address). AARP verifies the protocol destination node address of all packets received by a given node. It ensures that the destination address is either a broadcast address or the receiving node's protocol address. In short, AARP helps dispatch the packet to the correct hardware address and, for incoming packets, makes sure that the corresponding protocol address is correct for that physical node.

Address handling

The address handling process consists of assigning new addresses and actually mapping a protocol address to a hardware address.

Assigning new addresses

When a node is initialized, AARP assigns a unique protocol address for each protocol set running on the node. AARP can make this assignment, or the client can assign the addresses itself and then inform AARP.

The AARP approach takes three steps:

1. AARP assigns a tentative random address not already in the AMT.

2. AARP broadcasts probe packets to determine if any other node is using the address.

3. If it is not in use, the tentative address becomes permanent and AARP returns it to the client.

Otherwise, a receiving node notifies the probing node that the address is in use by returning a response packet. The probing node tries a new address, and repeats this process until it can return a valid address to its client.

Mapping addresses

The process of actually mapping a protocol address to a hardware address begins with a request from an AARP client. Upon receiving a request, AARP scans the AMT to see if the mapping is already there. If so, it returns the mapping information to the client. Otherwise, AARP initiates the following procedure:

1. It broadcasts a request packet that includes the protocol address for which mapping is required and the protocol set for mapping.

2. If a receiving node can match the protocol type to its protocol address, it returns a reply packet with the mapping information.

3. AARP enters this information in its AMT and passes it on to the client.

If the request packet does not induce a reply, AARP retransmits it a given number of times, after which it concludes that the node does not exist. AARP then returns an error message to the client. (The maximum number of times the request is transmitted is determined by the AARP developer.)

Examining incoming packets

Besides receiving and processing its own packets, AARP receives and examines all packets for any protocol set. By doing this, AARP can confirm that the incoming packets are correctly addressed. Examining each packet also allows AARP to glean address information and update the AMT.

Upon initialization, a client instructs AARP about how to receive and process the incoming packets. For example, the client might tell AARP to verify the address and then pass on or discard the packet.

Maintaining the Address Mapping Table (AMT)

An AMT contains the known set of corresponding hardware and protocol addresses. To keep an AMT current, AARP performs three maintenance operations on it:

- updating the table with new addresses
- removing unused addresses
- aging table entries

Whenever AARP establishes a new mapping, it updates the table to reflect the new address. Should the table become full, it removes unused addresses via a least-recently-used algorithm.

Two other problems remain, both having to do with the consequences of a node shutting down and a new node taking its address in its absence. This can cause the remaining nodes to have invalid addresses in their AMTs or to send replies to the wrong hardware address.

To prevent invalid entries, AARP can use a timer with each entry. Under timed aging, reception of a packet within a given time period causes an entry update or confirmation. If the timer expires before AARP receives a packet for an entry, it removes the entry from the AMT.

As another approach to avoid invalid entries, AARP can age-on-probe, removing an entry from the AMT upon receipt of a probe packet for the entry's protocol address. Although unnecessary removal can occur when a new node probes for an address that is already in use, age-on-probe guarantees that the AMT always contains the current mapping information.

Datagram Delivery Protocol (DDP)

The LocalTalk Link Access Protocol handles the delivery of information between nodes on a single network, and the Datagram Delivery Protocol (see *Figure 4-8*) extends this operation to delivery over an AppleTalk internet.

As discussed in Chapter 2, an internet consists of a number of networks linked together (see *Figure 4-9*). A router links one network to another. (Another device, a **gateway**, links dissimilar networks, translating the protocols between them.) DDP provides a way of delivering packets through the routers to another network. It does not include a mechanism to recover lost packets.

■ **Figure 4-8** Datagram Delivery Protocol (DDP)

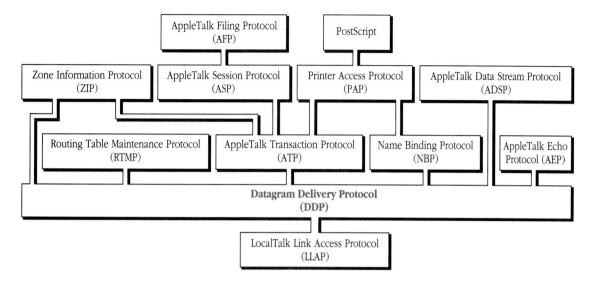

■ **Figure 4-9** AppleTalk internet and routers

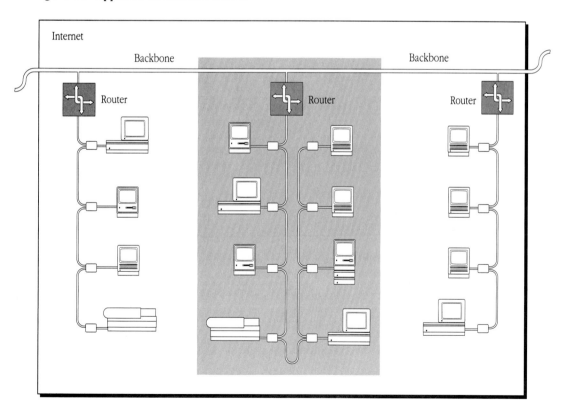

LLAP provides delivery of packets between nodes. DDP extends AppleTalk's addressing scheme to allow packets, called datagrams in DDP, to be sent to individual sockets within a single node (see *Figure 4-10*). The next section covers sockets in detail.

■ **Figure 4-10** DDP provides socket-to-socket delivery of packets (datagrams)

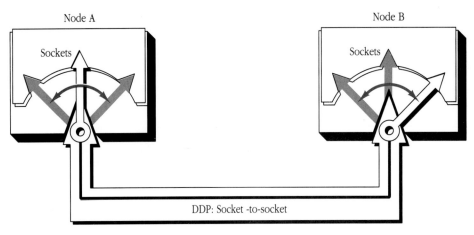

Within the datagram, a hop count field indicates the number of routers that the datagram has visited. An optional DDP checksum detects errors caused by faulty operation within internet routers. Typical problems include memory and data bus errors.

Sockets and socket clients

By using sockets, the AppleTalk system can address not only a simple node ID but also a specific part of a node. A socket is a logical addressable entity within a network node connected to an AppleTalk internet. Just as LLAP sends information to nodes within single networks, DDP directs information to sockets on an internet. A socket is owned by a **socket client,** which is typically a process implemented in software in the node. The client provides code, called its **socket listener,** that processes incoming datagrams.

On a single network, a socket's **AppleTalk address** is a combination of the socket's node ID and an 8-bit socket number that is unique within a given node. The socket numbers 1-127 are statically assigned, while the numbers 128-254 are dynamically assigned (see *Table 4-2*).

Socket numbers	Assignment	Purpose
1-63 ($01-$3F)	Static	Reserved by Apple
64-127 ($40-$7F)	Static	Unrestricted experimental use
128-254 ($80-$FE)	Dynamic	Send and receive datagrams between nodes

Socket numbers 1-63 are reserved for use by the core AppleTalk protocols. For more information on the dynamic socket number assignment process, refer to *Inside AppleTalk.*

A socket's internet address guarantees a unique identifier for a datagram's source and destination socket on an AppleTalk internet. An **internet address** consists of a socket's node ID and socket number (its AppleTalk address) and a network number. A **network number** is a unique 16-bit number that identifies a network in an internet. (A node also has an internet address, which consists of a node ID and a network number.)

Routing Table Maintenance Protocol (RTMP)

As discussed in the previous section, routers forward datagrams across an internet. A router uses RTMP (see *Figure 4-11*) to set up and maintain **routing tables** used to forward datagrams. To explain the operation of routing tables, this section covers:

■ router types

■ router operation

■ routing table setup

■ routing table maintenance

■ **Figure 4-11** Routing Table Maintenance Protocol (RTMP)

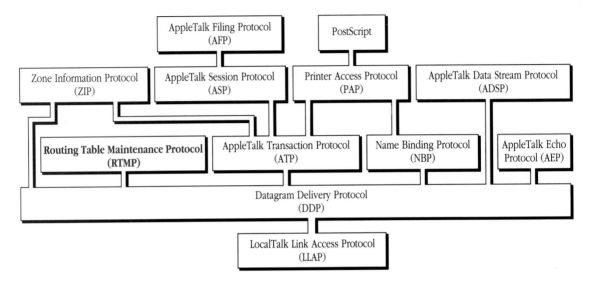

Router types

A router links a network to one or more additional like networks. Routers have multiple ports and forward data across the internet. The transition across a router to another network is called a hop. On an AppleTalk internet, a source node must be within 15 hops of the destination node, or communication will not occur. This limit helps filter out packets that may be circulating in a closed loop on the network. A closed loop can occur for a short time when routers are updating their routing tables.

Router configurations

The AppleTalk network system supports the following router configurations (see *Figure 4-12*):

■ Local router. A local router connects two or more networks in close proximity.

■ Half router. A half router is useful whenever remote networks are connected via long-distance links (such as telephone lines and modems). Here, each network is connected to a router, which in turn is connected to the data communications link. Thus, the router at each end serves as a "half router."

■ Backbone router. A backbone router is part of a set of routers that link multiple networks. It may have one or more ports connected as a local or half router, but it will also be connected to a backbone network.

■ **Figure 4-12** AppleTalk router configurations

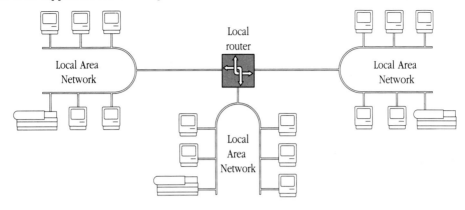

Local configuration

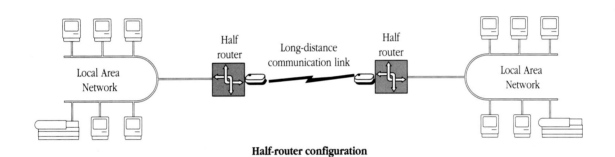

Half-router configuration

Backbone configuration

Router operation

A router contains several hardware ports. Routers accept datagrams from the link access protocol and direct them to their destination. Router internals (see *Figure 4-13*) include:

- a data link handler (LLAP or other) for each port
- a DDP routing process
- the routing table
- the routing table maintenance process

The router accepts datagrams from the data link handler, consults the routing table, and reroutes the packets through the appropriate port.

The hardware ports are called router ports, which can be connected in any of the three router configurations. However, within an internet, no two ports of any single router can be connected to the same local network.

- **Figure 4-13** Router model internals

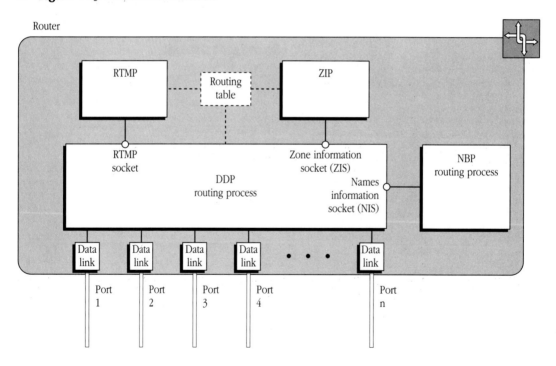

For each port, the router maintains a port descriptor, which consists of four fields:

- a connection status flag
- the port number
- the port node ID
- the port network number

The flag simply tells whether the port is connected to an AppleTalk network or some other type of network. The port number is assigned using administrative software and is not specified by RTMP. The port node ID is the router node ID for that port. (The node ID for a router is different for each port, meaning that the router acquires a different node ID for each network connected to it.) Finally, the port network number is the number of the specific network connected to the port.

The fields take on different meanings according to the configuration of the router (see *Table 4-3*). The fields used depend on the type of router.

■ **Table 4-3** Port descriptor fields and router configurations

Configuration	Flag	Port number	Port node ID	Port network number
Local router	✔	✔	✔	✔
Half router	✔	✔		
Backbone router	✔	✔	✔	

Routing table setup

A router maintains a routing table used in forwarding datagrams (see *Figure 4-14*). The routing table helps the router forward a datagram by identifying the port through which the router should send the datagram to reach the destination network. The routing table contains an entry for each network that a datagram can reach (that is, each one within 15 hops of the router).

Each entry includes:

- the port number for the destination network
- the node ID of the next router
- the distance in hops to the destination network

■ **Figure 4-14** Sample routing table

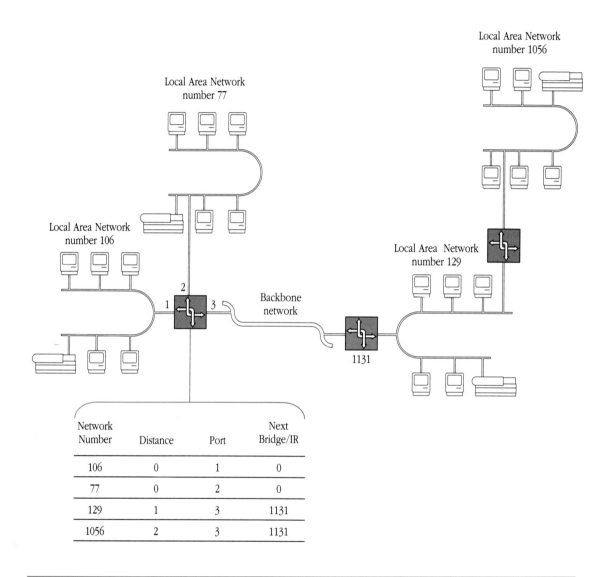

Network Number	Distance	Port	Next Bridge/IR
106	0	1	0
77	0	2	0
129	1	3	1131
1056	2	3	1131

Routing table maintenance

So that routers can continue to forward datagrams accurately, RTMP subjects routing tables to regular updates. This maintenance process allows the routing tables to adapt to the growth and change of an internet by keeping the tables current regarding the addition of new networks, route changes, and the removal of old networks or routers.

Essentially, the maintenance process works by having each router exchange routing tables with others in the internet on a regular basis, via the RTMP socket in each router. Each RTMP data packet includes a field called the **routing tuple,** which contains a network number and the distance travelled in hops from the router to that network. The router compares the incoming tuples with the current entries in its routing table and adds any new networks to the table. The tables are also adjusted for changes in distance to existing networks.

To remove networks from the table, RTMP assumes that all entries are valid for a limited time and regularly starts a validity timer to age entries. Before starting the timer, RTMP changes the status of all entries in a router's table from "good" to "suspect." If the router does not receive an RTMP packet to revalidate an entry in the table before the timer expires, it changes the status of those nonreporting entries to "bad." (The other entries revert to "good.") If the entry remains "bad" after the next timer cycle, RTMP removes it from the table.

AppleTalk Echo Protocol (AEP)

The AppleTalk Echo Protocol (see *Figure 4-15*) allows any node to send a datagram and to receive an "echoed" copy in return. With echoing, an AEP client can estimate the round trip time for a typical packet to a remote node (such as a server) and determine if a node with echoing capabilities is accessible over the network.

Echoing can be used only with those clients that have an echoer process on a particular statically assigned socket (socket 4). The echoer determines whether a packet should be echoed by examining all packets received through this socket, looking for a DDP protocol type of 4 and a data length of a least one byte. For these packets, the echoer:

1. checks for an echo header (the first byte must equal 1, which signifies an echo request)

2. changes the value to 2 (for echo reply)

3. calls DDP to return the packet to its sender, through the originating socket

The echoer discards all other packets.

■ **Figure 4-15** AppleTalk Echo Protocol (AEP)

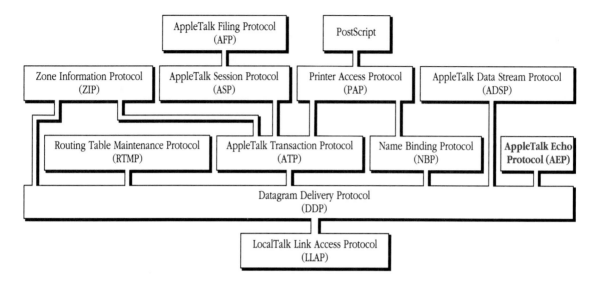

The AppleTalk Echo Protocol client will not receive an echo reply if

■ the AppleTalk Echo Protocol packets are lost in the internet

■ the target node does not have an echoer

■ the target node is unreachable or down

The client itself determines how long to wait or how many times to retry the echo request before concluding that one of these conditions has occurred.

Name Binding Protocol (NBP)

While the AppleTalk protocols use numeric identifiers to address entities on a network, users can remember names more easily. In order to use entity names, the Name Binding Protocol (see *Figure 4-16*) provides a means of converting a named address into the numeric address required by the other protocols.

■ **Figure 4-16** Name Binding Protocol (NBP)

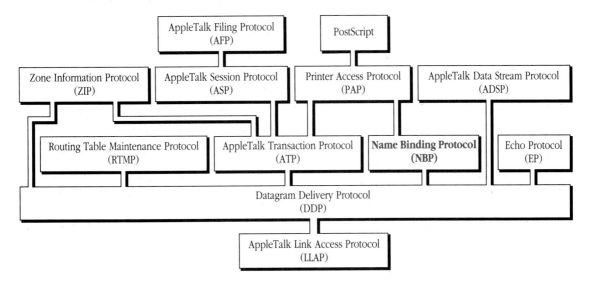

NBP is important in dynamic node ID assignment, because a node's AppleTalk (numeric) address can change, but a named address usually remains the same. Understanding the concepts of entity names and name binding helps make the workings of NBP more apparent.

Entity names

Entity is short for **network-visible entity,** which refers to any entity that is accessible over an AppleTalk network system through DDP. Under this definition, nodes are not network-visible; rather, it is the services within the nodes — as represented by the socket clients — that are visible.

For example, a printer is not network-visible, but the print service is. The print service is typically a socket client on what might be called the print server's request listening socket. Similarly, a user on the network is not network visible, but the user's electronic mailbox is because it has an internet address.

An NBP tuple contains the entity name, its 4-byte internet address, and a 1-byte enumerator. The enumerator is used in cases when more than one entity name is registered on a single socket.

A network-visible entity can assign an **entity name** to itself. An entity name contains three fields of up to 32 characters each in the following form:

object:type@zone

For example:

Robinson:Mailbox@Kentwood East

Here, "Robinson" is the object (presumably the user) and "Mailbox" represents the entity type. This particular mailbox is located in an internet zone named "Kentwood East". Thus, the object field represents the name, and the type and zone fields qualify it. All fields are case insensitive; spaces may be used in the names, however spaces are significant.

Zones are discussed fully in the "Zone Information Protocol" section, but basically they represent groups of networks on an internet.

Certain wildcards are valid in the name fields when used in place of the entire name:

■ In the object and type fields, an equal sign (=) means "any".

■ In the zone field, an asterisk (*) represents the zone in which the requesting node resides.

For example,

=:Mailbox@*

signifies all named mailboxes in the requester's zone. Similarly,

Robinson:=@*

asks for all entities named Robinson in the requester's zone, regardless of type.

Name binding

Name binding is the process by which a client obtains the address of a named entity (see *Figure 4-17*). The name binding process maps an entity name to its internet address.

■ **Figure 4-17** Name binding process

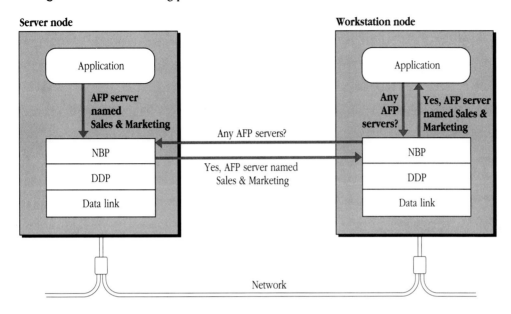

Each node maintains a **names table** containing name-to-entity internet address mappings of all named socket clients that reside in that node. Since NBP allows an entity to have more than one name, aliases and enumerators are stored in a names table as applicable. A **names directory** is a distributed database that contains the name-to-address mappings of all nodes on the internet. NBP uses the names directory to provide the name binding services of name registration, name deletion, name lookup, and name confirmation.

Moreover, each node implements NBP on a statically assigned socket (socket 2) called the names information socket. NBP maintains the names table and handles name lookup requests.

Services

NBP provides four basic services:

■ name registration

■ name deletion

■ name lookup

■ name confirmation

Name registration occurs when an entity enters its name and socket number into the names directory. Conversely, **name deletion** means that an entity has removed its name and socket number from the names directory. **Name lookup** refers to the actual binding of a name to its internet address. **Name confirmation** checks and validates the current binding.

The success of these services depends on several factors. Name registration fails if an entity enters a name already in use, an invalid name, or an invalid socket number. Name deletion, name lookup, and name confirmation fail if NBP cannot find the entity name.

NBP on a single network

On a single network, mapping a name involves three steps:

1. The requesting node's NBP broadcasts an NBP lookup packet. Addressed to the names information socket (NIS), a lookup packet carries the entity name to be looked up.

2. Each node's NBP process receives the lookup request and searches its names table for a match of the name.

3. If a match is found, NBP sends a lookup reply to the requesting socket, along with the entity name's address.

These steps may be repeated to recover from lost request or response packets. If no match is found, the lookup packet is ignored, and NBP in the requesting node concludes that no entity is using that name.

NBP on an internet

The lookup process on an internet is the same, with two preceding steps:

1. The requesting socket sends a directed NBP Broadcast Request packet. Addressed to the NIS of any router on the requester's network, a Broadcast Request carries the entity name to be looked up.

2. The router's NBP process receives the Broadcast Request and sends a broadcast lookup request for each network in the target zone.

The lookup process then proceeds as it does on a single network, starting with the second step.

Zone Information Protocol (ZIP)

A zone is a grouping of networks in an internet that facilitate the departmental grouping of network resources. In AppleTalk, zones have the following characteristics:

- An AppleTalk zone consists of a collection of AppleTalk networks.

- A particular AppleTalk network belongs to exactly one zone.

- The networks of a particular zone need not be directly connected.

- All the zones together make up the entire internet.

NBP uses ZIP (see *Figure 4-18*) to determine which networks belong to which zones. Routers use ZIP to maintain the network-number-to-zone-name mapping of the internet. ZIP also provides maintenance commands so nodes that are not routers can obtain the current mapping and network administrators can change the mapping as needed.

- **Figure 4-18** Zone Information Protocol (ZIP)

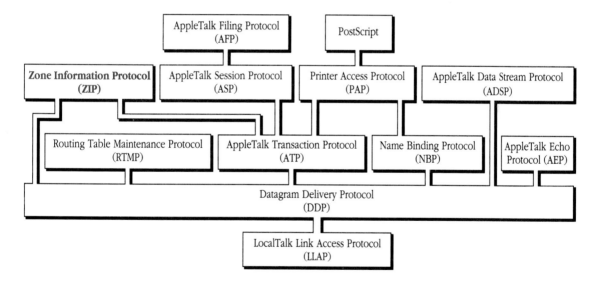

Network-to-zone mapping

ZIP uses a data structure called the **zone information table (ZIT).** A ZIT resides in each router together with the routing table. It provides a listing of network numbers for each network in every zone. An individual entry is a tuple matching a single network number with its zone name, which is supplied by the network administrator.

Routers send requests for zone information to other routers through the statically assigned zone information socket (ZIS). These zone queries contain a list of network numbers for which the requesting numbers require a zone name. The router sends a zone reply back through the ZIS; the zone reply lists the zone names known to the router.

ZIP monitors the routing table to determine if a new network has been added or if a network has gone down. If a network goes down, ZIP deletes the corresponding table entry from the ZIT. The network may return later with a different zone name assigned. In this case, or in the case of a wholly new network, ZIP adds a table entry to the ZIT.

Upon detecting a new network, ZIP adds an entry for it to the zone information table and sends out a timed query to discover the network's zone name. When it receives the name in a zone reply, ZIP adds the new name to the table. When the timer expires, ZIP retransmits one query for each remaining unknown zone. Eventually, on a stable internet, the ZIT in every router will contain the entire network-to-zone mapping and further ZIP activity will rarely occur.

Changing and listing zones

To change a zone name, ZIP combines with RTMP to essentially "bring down" the network. Once down, a network's entry disappears from all of the routing tables in all of the routers on the internet. At the same time, ZIP removes the network's entry from the zone information tables in all routers. ZIP and RTMP then bring the network back up with the new zone name. The new name propagates across the internet via the zone query process, and the network becomes associated with its new zone name.

Nodes that are not routers can obtain the name of any zone on an internet by sending out ZIP queries. Since a zone query is a best-effort process, the requesting node must also implement a timeout-and-retry mechanism. A nonrouter node can use other ZIP commands to obtain a list of all zones on an internet and to determine its own zone name. (This may not produce a correct response if the zone name is in the process of being changed.)

AppleTalk Transaction Protocol (ATP)

Transport protocols ensure the loss-free delivery of DDP client packets from source to destination. The AppleTalk Transaction Protocol (see *Figure 4-19*) satisfies the transport needs of network peripheral devices and fulfills the transaction needs for additional general networking.

■ **Figure 4-19** AppleTalk Transaction Protocol (ATP)

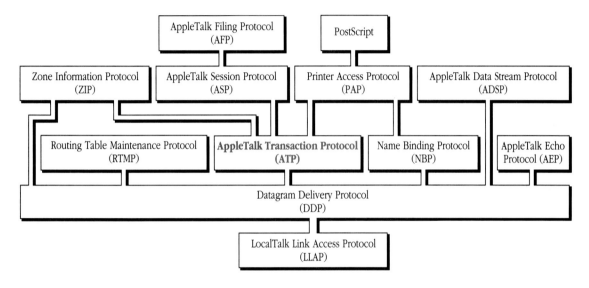

ATP transactions

During an ATP transaction between socket clients (see *Figure 4-20*), one client asks the other to perform a higher-level action and report the outcome. The other client then responds accordingly. The request for action is called a **transaction request,** and the report of the action is the **transaction response.**

■ **Figure 4-20** ATP transaction

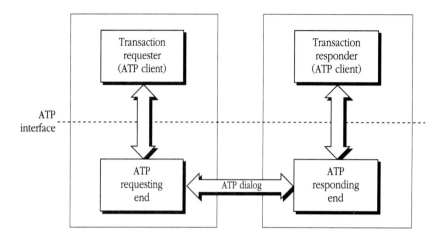

A transaction identifier (TID) sent with each request allows the ATP requesting client to distinguish between several outstanding responses. The ATP responding client includes the TID with the response; the requester can then match the response to the original request.

Since ATP limits a request to a single packet, a response message may require several packets. The responder sends these sequentially; the transaction is complete when the requester receives all of them. ATP then delivers the response as a single entity to the requester.

Error recovery

An ATP transaction is performed in the face of three possible error conditions:

■ the transaction request is lost in the network

■ the transaction response is lost or delayed in the network

■ the responder becomes unreachable

To attempt to recover from any of these conditions, ATP on the requesting end starts a timer. If the timer expires before a response is received, ATP retransmits the request (see *Figure 4-21*). ATP continues retransmitting until it gets a response or until it reaches a maximum retry count. If it is still unable to reach the responder, ATP concludes that the responder is unreachable and notifies the requester.

■ **Figure 4-21** ATP error recovery procedure

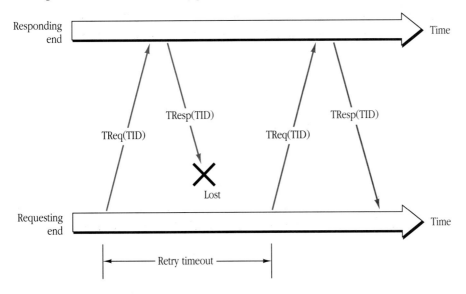

An ATP transaction takes one of two forms:

■ an at-least-once transaction

■ an exactly-once transaction

At-least-once transactions

As its name suggests, an **at-least-once transaction (ALO)** is executed at least one time, possibly several times. The requester chooses an ALO transaction if repeated execution of the request provides the same result as executing it once (for example, asking a destination to identify itself). Since the requester can be certain that the result will not change upon a retry, there is no concern if it becomes necessary to retransmit the request.

Exactly-once transactions

The ATP error recovery mechanism may cause a request to be retransmitted. This can cause serious damage if the request can receive different results each time it is transmitted. In this case, the requester can initiate an **exactly-once transaction (XO),** which will be delivered to the ATP responding-end client only once, if at all.

ATP performs XO transactions by filtering duplicate requests in the responding end using a list of recently received transactions. The XO transaction process works this way (see *Figure 4-22*):

1. The ATP responding client receives a request to perform some action.

2. ATP on the responding inserts the new request into the transaction list, and the responder executes it.

3. The responder then issues its reply to the requester, and ATP attaches a copy of the reply to the transaction's entry in the list.

4. When the requestor receives the response, ATP on the requesting end returns a transaction release packet to the responder.

5. When the responder receives the transaction release packet, ATP removes the request from the transaction list.

Note that until the responder has received a transaction release packet and ATP has removed the request, a copy of the original request remains available in the responder's transaction list. If the same request comes in while the original request remains in the transaction list, ATP will not pass along the repeated request to the ATP responding end client.

Exactly-Once transactions are not guaranteed in all environments because of the presence of multiple paths from source to destination and varying delays on those paths. Refer to *Inside AppleTalk* for more information on XO transactions.

■ **Figure 4-22** ATP exactly-once service transactions

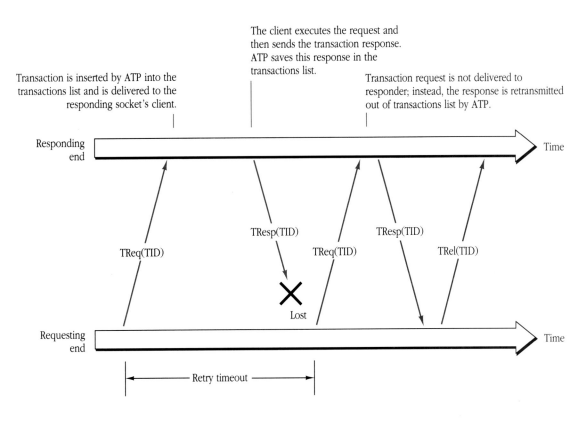

Transaction is inserted by ATP into the transactions list and is delivered to the responding socket's client.

The client executes the request and then sends the transaction response. ATP saves this response in the transactions list.

Transaction request is not delivered to responder; instead, the response is retransmitted out of transactions list by ATP.

Responding end — Time

TResp(TID)   TResp(TID)

TReq(TID)   TReq(TID)   TRel(TID)

✗
Lost

Requesting end — Time

├—— Retry timeout ——┤

Printer Access Protocol (PAP)

The Printer Access Protocol (see *Figure 4-23*) establishes communications between a workstation and a print server by performing connection setup, maintenance, and teardown operations in addition to data transfer. Once a connection is opened to the server, the PAP client at either end can receive data from or write data to the other end. PAP uses NBP and ATP services to find addresses and send data.

■ **Figure 4-23** Printer Access Protocol (PAP)

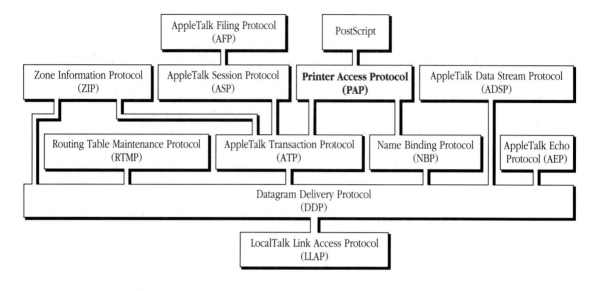

Workstation-printer connection

PAP's functions involve five basic procedures:

■ opening a connection

■ transferring data

■ closing a connection

■ determining a print server's status

■ filtering duplicate requests

PAP calls NBP to obtain the address of the server's session listening socket (SLS). Clients can exchange data only after the workstation opens a connection to the print server.

With the connection open, the clients exchange data. A connection timer of two minutes at each end allows PAP to detect half-open connections, where one end is established but the other is closed. If the timer expires without receiving a packet from the other end, PAP closes the connection. Upon completion of the data transfer, either end can close the connection.

The remaining two operations fill maintenance roles. The workstation can determine the status of the print server at any time, regardless of whether a connection is open.

As for duplicate filtration, recall that ATP XO transactions cannot guarantee exactly-once delivery of requests. PAP uses a sequence number to detect and ignore duplicates.

AppleTalk Session Protocol (ASP)

The AppleTalk Session Protocol (see *Figure 4-24*) provides a method for passing commands between a workstation and a server during a **session**, that is, when there is a connection between a workstation and server. ASP ensures that the commands are delivered without duplication in the same order as they were sent and conveys the results of these commands back to the workstation. As stated earlier, the AppleTalk Transaction Protocol (ATP) provides a reliable transaction service; ASP builds upon ATP's services to provide the level of transport service needed for higher-level workstation-to-server interaction.

ASP provides four basic services: opening a session, closing a session, session request handling, and session management.

■ **Figure 4-24** AppleTalk Session Protocol (ASP)

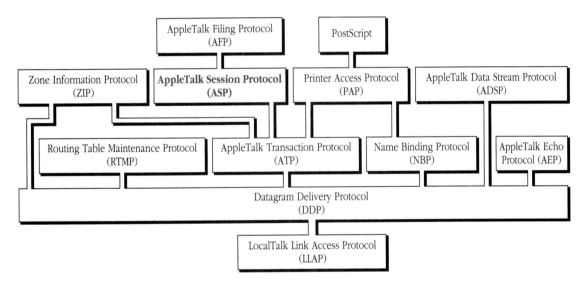

Opening a session

Two steps must be performed prior to a workstation's opening a session with a server:

■ Both the workstation and the server must query ASP to ascertain the maximum allowable command and reply sizes.

■ The workstation must obtain the address of the server's session listening socket by issuing a call to NBP.

The session listening socket is a responding socket opened by ASP through which the server makes itself known on the network.

After identifying the address of the intended server's SLS (see *Figure 4-25*):

1. The workstation client asks ASP to open a session with a particular server.

2. ASP sends an OpenSess packet to the server's SLS. This packet carries the address of the workstation session socket (WSS).

3. If the server is able to establish a session, it responds with a session acceptance indicator, the session identifier, and the address of the server session socket (SSS).

■ **Figure 4-25** Opening a session

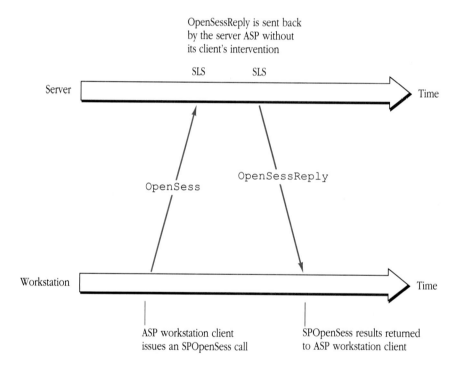

The workstation session socket receives the tickle packets described below in the "Session Management" section. The server session socket name implies that it receives all future communication on that particular session from the workstation.

Closing a session

Either end of the connection can close a session. The workstation closes a session by sending a command to the SSS (see *Figure 4-26*). The server closes a session by sending a command to the WSS (see *Figure 4-27*). After a session is closed, the respective ASP clients must be notified.

■ **Figure 4-26** Closing a session (initiated by workstation)

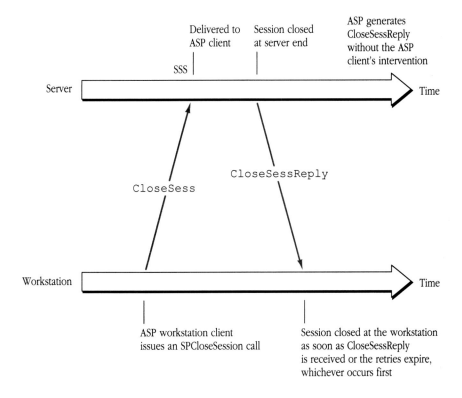

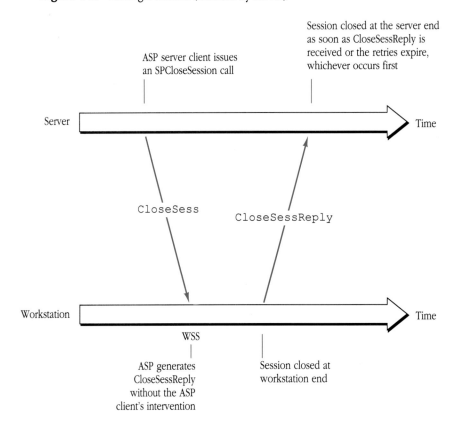

Session request handling

ASP serves as a vehicle for conveying commands and replies between workstation and server. The commands and replies translate into ATP transaction requests and responses. ASP requests take three forms:

■ commands

■ writes

■ attention requests

An ASP command instructs the server to perform a function and return a reply to the workstation (see *Figure 4-28*). A command translates into an ATP request to the SSS. The reply, which includes the result of the command, takes the form of an ATP response.

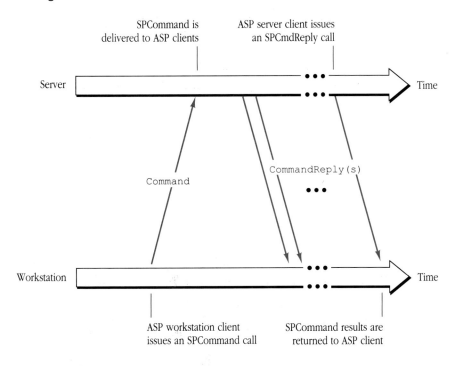

■ **Figure 4-28** ASP command transaction

For example, the workstation may command the server to open a file or read a range of bytes in a file. The latter example could well result in a multipacket response. (Recall that ATP sends multipacket responses sequentially and delivers them as a single reply.)

During an ASP write, the workstation transports a block of data via ATP to the server, along with a request for a reply (see *Figure 4-29*). Essentially, ASP transports data to the server by asking the server to read it from the workstation. ASP acts on the block of data in this manner:

1. ASP sends an ATP request to the server session socket.

2. The server examines the request to determine whether or not to proceed with reading the data from the workstation.

3. If the server does not wish to proceed, it returns an error.

4. If the server wishes to proceed, it issues a request to read information from the workstation server socket.

5. The server processes the data and replies.

If for some reason the server cannot handle the request, it returns an error message to the workstation client.

■ **Figure 4-29** ASP write transaction

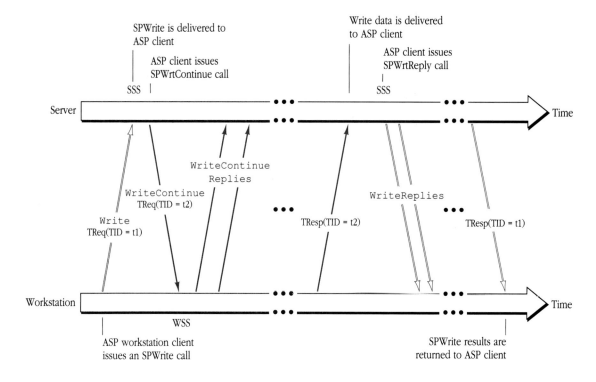

An attention request (which is an ATP at-least-once transaction) is a request from the server to the workstation that alerts the workstation client that the server requires some sort of attention. For example, a server may wish to alert a workstation to a change in the server's status. The workstation would find out the details of the status change via an ASP request to the server.

Session management

ASP manages a session using specific processes:

■ tickling

■ duplicate filtration

■ packet sequencing

Session tickling is a process by which each end periodically informs the other that it remains open by sending special tickle packets to the other end. If one end does not receive any tickle packets from the other within a given time period, it assumes that the other end has either gone down or become otherwise unreachable. The open end then closes the session.

To perform duplicate filtration, ASP takes a similar approach to PAP, giving each packet a sequence number. The presence of a sequence number in each packet means that a series of commands and writes will be received in the same order that they were issued, even across an internet. Sequence numbers also ensure that the receiving end does not process duplicate packets, because a packet is discarded if its sequence number is the same as a previously received packet.

AppleTalk Data Stream Protocol (ADSP)

ADSP (see *Figure 4-30*) guarantees sequential, full-duplex, duplicate-free delivery of bytes between two communicating entities on an AppleTalk internet. The sending client uses ADSP to break up the data stream into logical messages that the receiving client can understand. Using ADSP, a client can open a connection with another end, exchange data with the other end, and close the connection.

■ **Figure 4-30** AppleTalk Data Stream Protocol (ADSP)

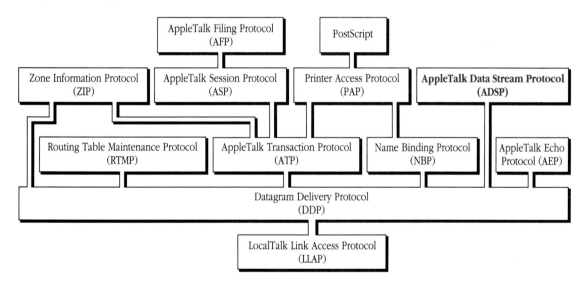

To augment stream delivery, ADSP provides services for sending reliable attention messages and forward resets. An attention message is a means for the clients of the two connection ends to signal each other without disrupting the normal flow of data. These messages are delivered reliably, in order, and free of duplication. With a forward reset, an ADSP client can stop delivery of any outstanding data to the remote end's client. A forward reset resynchronizes the two ends after discarding all bytes in the sending end's send queue, all bytes in transit on the network, and all bytes that have not yet been delivered to the client.

The connection-opening mechanism, which is covered in the next section, provides a symmetric connection opening between sockets.

ADSP tasks

The full-duplex, byte-stream service provided by ADSP performs three fundamental tasks:

■ connecting sockets

■ data sequencing

■ packet sequencing

A **connection** is an association between two sockets that allows reliable, full-duplex flow of data between the sockets. **Data sequencing** ensures the orderly, sequential flow of data between connections; similarly, **packet sequencing** ensures that packets are received in the correct order.

ADSP connections

With ADSP, data bytes are delivered in the same order as they are inserted into the connection. Moreover, a flow control mechanism is built into the protocol, regulating data transmission based on the availability of reception buffers at the destination to prevent a sender from "flooding" a receiver.

A connection itself can be open, half open, or closed (see *Table 4-4*). Collectively, these are known as the **connection states.** A connection is open when both connections ends are established; a half-open connection has one end established and the other closed. A closed connection has both ends closed. Data flows on a connection only if it is open.

Connection end state		Connection state
Connection end A	**Connection end B**	
closed	closed	closed
established	closed	half open
closed	established	half open
established	established	open

Opening a connection

To open a connection, ADSP provides a control packet known as an Open Connection Request packet. The end initiating the connection starts a connection dialog with the intended remote end by sending this packet (see *Figure 4-31*). The packet provides the remote end with connection parameters it needs to become established. Once the remote end has set these parameters, the connection end is established.

■ **Figure 4-31** Connection-opening dialog initiated by *one* end

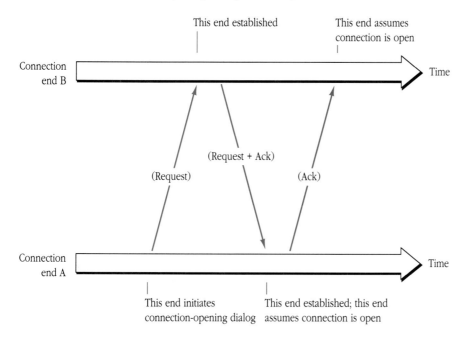

At this point, the connection is only half open; to become fully open, both ends must be established. Therefore, the remote end also sends an Open Connection Request packet to the originating end. Only after the originating end establishes its connection is the connection fully open. If for any reason an ADSP implementation cannot fulfill the open-connection request, an open-connection denial is sent back to the requester.

Both ends can initiate a connection simultaneously (see *Figure 4-32*).

■ **Figure 4-32** Connection-opening dialog initiated by *both* ends

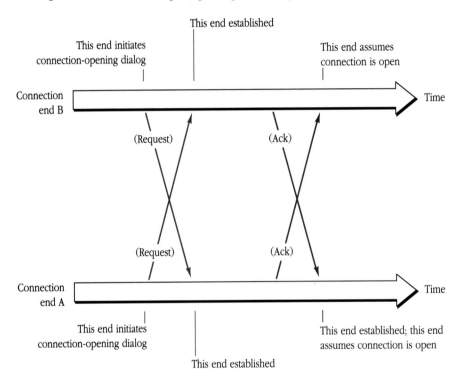

Closing a connection

ADSP closes a connection when

- either end determines that, because the other end does not respond to repeated probes, it is either down or unreachable
- the client at either end uses ADSP to close the connection

In the first case, ADSP immediately closes down the remote connection and notifies the local end's client that the connection is closed. In the second case, which can occur at any time, the local connection end's ADSP awaits acknowledgment of the delivery of any outstanding bytes in its send queue before closing the connection.

Before closing an open connection, ADSP sends a Close Connection Advice control packet to the remote end. Upon receiving it, the remote end ADSP verifies that the packet is properly sequenced. If the packet has arrived out of sequence, the receiving end may discard or buffer it until the arrival of any intervening data packets. This avoids prematurely closing the connection while data packets are delayed in internet routers. Once the Close Connection Advice control packet is accepted, ADSP closes that connection end and informs the client of the change in status.

◆ *Note:* The Close Connection Advice control packet is sent automatically, but its delivery is not guaranteed. If the packet is not successfully delivered to the remote end, the remote end will eventually time out and tear down the connection.

Detecting half-open connections

To prevent needless consumption of network resources, ADSP detects and completely closes any half-open connections. Therefore, each connection end maintains a connection timer that is started when the connection opens. The timer is reset for each incoming packet received from the remote end; it expires if no packet arrives within 30 seconds. This initiates the process of detecting and closing a half-open connection:

1. The receiving end resets the timer and sends a probe request to the remote end for acknowledgment. (The probe itself serves as an acknowledgment to the remote end.)

2. Failure to receive any packet from the other end before the timer expires for the fourth time indicates that the connection is half open.

3. ADSP immediately closes the open end, freeing all associated resources.

Connection identifiers

A connection end is identified by its internet socket address and by a 16-bit connection identifier. Recall that an internet socket address consists of a socket number, node ID, and network number. When a connection is established, each end generates a 16-bit number known as its connection identifier (CID). A sender must include its CID in all packets.

This means that a connection is uniquely identified by the internet address and the CID of either end. Including the CID avoids identification problems otherwise caused by the rapid opening and closing of connections and by packets from older connections between the same connection ends.

Data sequencing

To ensure the orderly, sequential flow of data between connections, ADSP uses a technique called data sequencing. Data sequencing associates a 32-bit sequence number with each byte sent on the connection in a particular direction. The first byte sent has the sequence number 0, the next byte has 1, and so on. When the sequence number reaches $FFFFFFFF, it starts back at 0.

Packet sequencing

To ensure that packets are received in the correct order, ADSP uses a technique called packet sequencing. To carry out packet sequencing, each ADSP packet carries a number known as a PktFirstByteSeq. This is the sequence number of the first data byte in the packet. The PktFirstByteSeq is used during data acceptance, which is discussed in the next section.

Data flow

Four processes help maintain the orderly flow of data:

- data acceptance
- data acknowledgment
- error recovery
- flow control

Data acceptance is the process by which the receiving end accepts data from the sending end. ADSP uses a receiver variable named RecvSeq to keep track of data acceptance. RecvSeq is the sequence number of the next data byte that the receiver expects to receive from the other end and is generally equal to the sequence number of the last byte received plus one.

Upon receiving a data packet, the receiver compares PktFirstByteSeq with its own RecvSeq. If the numbers coincide, the receiver accepts the packet; otherwise, it discards the packet. After receiving an acceptable packet, the receiver advances its own RecvSeq number to the next expected number.

The RecvSeq number also assists in **data acknowledgment,** whereby the receiver confirms the acceptance of valid data. The receiving end simply returns its RecvSeq value to the sending end using a field called PktNextRecvSeq in any ADSP packet.

ADSP puts in place an error recovery mechanism that takes effect whenever the receiver rejects an incoming data packet (see *Figure 4-33*). For all unacknowledged packets, the sender saves the FirstRtmtSeq number and maintains a retry timer. FirstRtmtSeq is the sequence number of the oldest byte sent that remains unacknowledged. When the retry timer expires, the sender retransmits unacknowledged data bytes, starting with the sequence number FirstRtmtSeq.

■ **Figure 4-33** ADSP error recovery

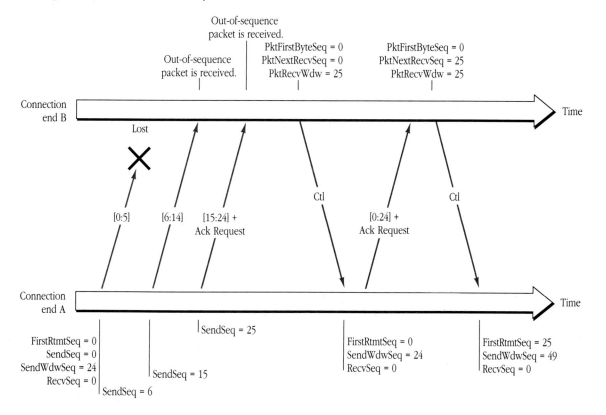

Finally, ADSP implements **flow control** to ensure that one end does not transmit data that the other end does not have enough buffer space to receive. To make this work, the receiving end periodically updates the sending end as to the amount of available buffer space by informing the sending end of the current reception window size.

Under flow control, each end maintains variables named RecvWdw and SendWdwSeq. RecvWdw is equal to the buffer size (in bytes) that one end has for receiving data from the other end. This value is included in all outgoing ADSP packets in a field called PktRecvWdw. SendWdwSeq represents the sequence number of the last byte for which the opposite end currently has space; that is, it signifies the last known buffer size. The connection ends keep this value current by adding the value of PktRecvWdw to the value of PktNextRecvSeq (the RecvSeq value as contained in an ADSP packet).

Summary of sequencing variables

To summarize, ADSP uses three sequence variables:

PktFirstByteSeq	The sequence number of the packet's first data byte
PktNextRecvSeq	The sequence number of the next byte that the packet's sender expects to receive
PktRecvWdw	The number of bytes that the packet's sender currently has buffer space to receive

Each connection end must maintain the following variables as part of its connection state descriptor:

SendSeq	The sequence number to be assigned to the next new byte that the local end will transmit over the connection
FirstRtmtSeq	The sequence number of the oldest byte in the local end's send queue (initially, the queue is empty; subsequently, this number equals SendSeq)
SendWdwSeq	The sequence number of the last byte that the remote end has buffer space to receive
RecvSeq	The sequence number of the next byte the local end expects to receive
RecvWdw	The number of bytes that the local end currently has buffer space to receive (initially, the entire buffer is available)

Data flow example

Figure 4-34 illustrates data flow on an ADSP connection, showing specifically how the ADSP variables relate to the flow of data. As the figure shows, End A sends data and control packets to End B, which receives them and returns acknowledgments to End A. The same applies to the reverse situation of End B sending packets to End A, save for the sending of acknowledgments. Acknowledgments are implicit in all packets sent from End B, regardless of whether they are data packets or control packets.

■ **Figure 4-34** ADSP data flow

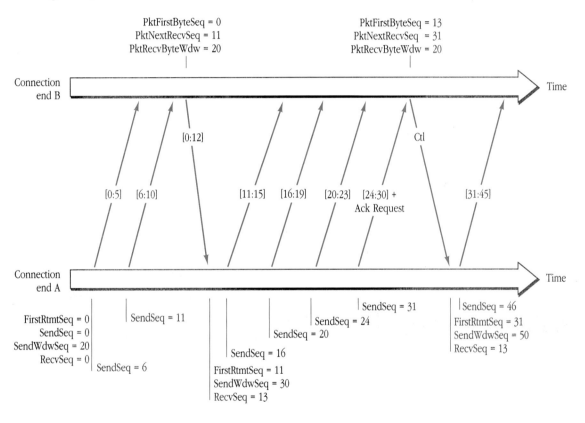

In Figure 4-33 and 4-34, the packets are indicated by arrows that run diagonally between the two connection ends. The bracketed ranges (for example, [0:5]) indicate the range of sequence numbers assigned to data bytes transmitted in the packet. The first number in the range corresponds to PktFirstByteSeq. *Ctl* indicates Control packets. A vertical line above or below the time arrows indicates an event, either the transmission or reception of a packet. The values of variables before an event occurs are shown on the left side of the vertical line; values after the event are shown on the right side. The packet variables of all packets sent by connection End B are listed along End B's time axis.

AppleTalk Filing Protocol (AFP)

A workstation program manipulates files on a local disk by using its native file system commands. Through AFP (see *Figure 4-35*), a workstation program can use the same native file system commands to manipulate files on a shared disk that resides on a different node, known as a file server.

■ **Figure 4-35** AppleTalk Filing Protocol (AFP)

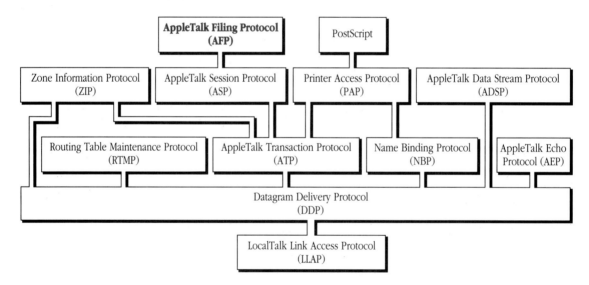

AFP within AppleTalk

To share information or files, a file server and a workstation must first use other AppleTalk protocols to establish a logical connection. AFP is a client of ASP, using ASP to open the connection, called a session, which allows protocol information to pass between two network devices such as a workstation and file server.

Before a session can be opened, the workstation must know the address of the server's session listening socket (SLS). To obtain an SLS, the server uses the AppleTalk Transaction Protocol (ATP). Then, the server uses the Name Binding Protocol (NBP) to register the file server's name and type on the socket.

Once the server has opened the SLS and registered the file server's name, file service is available to workstations. To use the file server, a workstation first calls NBP to look up the file server's name and obtain its address. With this information, the workstation then uses ASP to open a session.

After a session with the server is established, the workstation issues an AFP command to log on. Once the log-on process is complete, the workstation and the server may exchange AFP calls. The directory access rights and the file access and deny modes determine the level of access that the workstation user has to the server. When the workstation is finished, it logs off to end the session. Security procedures are available; they are covered in the section "AFP security."

AFP is extensible, meaning that later versions build upon the services of earlier versions, so a server may recognize several different versions of AFP. During the log-on process, the server sends to the workstation a list of AFP versions that it recognizes, and the workstation chooses which version to use.

File access

The definition of AFP includes a file access model (see *Figure 4-36*) that allows file sharing among nodes with different native file systems. (Macintosh, Apple II, and PC workstations each have distinct native file systems.) The native file system commands are automatically sent through the AFP Translator, where they are converted into AFP calls. The AFP calls are then transmitted across the network.

■ **Figure 4-36** AFP file access model

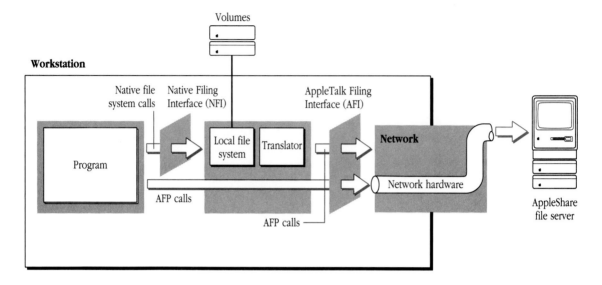

Volumes

Workstation

Native file / Native Filing   AppleTalk Filing
system calls / Interface (NFI)   Interface (AFI)

Program

Local file / Translator
system

Network

Network hardware

AFP calls

AFP calls

AppleShare
file server

The applications programmer must design the translator for the native file system that will access the file server. However, Apple has already designed translators for the Macintosh, Apple II, and MS-DOS file systems. A workstation application can make AFP calls directly, bypassing the translator, if the workstation needs to send a call that has no equivalent command in its native file system.

File structure

The AFP file structure enables user applications to share files using AFP calls. The file structure is made up of entities that are addressable through AFP, such as file servers, volumes, directories, files, and forks; AFP specifies the relationships between these entities.

Each entity has identifying parameters which are used in the AFP calls. For more information on these parameters, refer to *Inside AppleTalk*.

File servers

A file server is a device that provides a central storage area where workstations on a network can access files and applications. The file server is a computer with at least one large-capacity disk, called a volume. Multiple servers are allowed on a network; each server has a unique name and other identifying parameters that permit a workstation to find a particular server on the network.

Volumes

A file server can make one or more volumes available to the workstations on the network. As with the file server, each volume has identifying parameters. Additionally, the server can maintain an optional password parameter to provide security at the level of each volume.

Directories and files

Directories and files are stored in volumes, which are arranged in a branching tree structure. The **volume catalog** describes this hierarchical volume structure (see *Figure 4-37*). In this tree structure, all branching begins at a base directory called the root.

Files and directories within the tree are referred to as catalog nodes or CNodes. CNodes have a parent/offspring relationship: a given CNode is the offspring of the CNode above it in the catalog tree, and the higher CNode is considered its parent.

Directories in the tree may branch to files and other directories. To reach any point in the tree, each directory has an identifier through which it and its offspring can be addressed. Other parameters associated with files and directories define specific characteristics, such as file size and directory access privileges.

File forks

In the AFP file access model as well as the Macintosh file system, a file consists of two **forks:** a resource fork and a data fork. The resource fork holds Macintosh operating system resources, such as icons and windows, while the data fork contains the actual file data in an unstructured sequence. AFP treats both forks as finite-length byte sequences.

A file can have one or both forks empty. Non-Macintosh computers that require only one fork must use the data fork. A PC workstation accessing a file created on a Macintosh should not be concerned with the resource fork, since its function is not applicable to a non-Macintosh machine. Consequently, a PC workstation should never alter the contents of the resource fork, as the Macintosh expects that fork to contain system resources.

To read or write to the contents of a file's data or resource fork, the workstation issues a call to open that particular fork. This creates an access path to the fork, and all subsequent read and write calls refer to it through a specific parameter while the fork remains open.

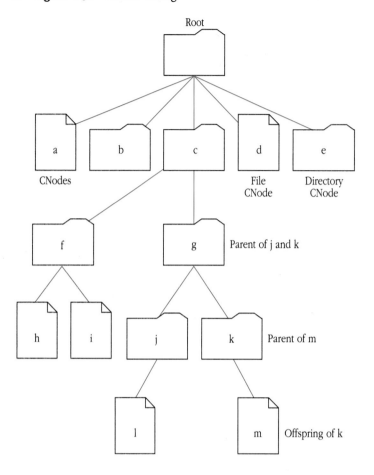

AFP security

Information stored in a shared resource needs protection from unauthorized users. AFP provides network security in three ways. It performs user authentication when a user logs on to the server sets up an optional volume password when a user first attempts to gain access to a volume, and provides directory access controls based on user authentication when a user logs on.

AFP provides three classes of **user authentication methods.** The first is no user authentication. The other two require sending information to the server. Cleartext password transmits to the server the user name and password as cleartext. The most secure method, random number exchange, sends an encrypted random number based on the password over the network.

Volume passwords provide an optional second level of access control. If the volume has a password, the user must give the password with the volume identifier before access to the volume is granted.

Directory access controls restrict the access rights of users. Users may have rights to search, read, and/or write to a directory's contents. Search access allows users to list the parameters of directories within a directory. A directory's parameters include its long and short name, parent IDs, and any associated access rights. A user with read access can list the parameters of files within the directory and read the contents of files in the directory. A file's parameters include its long and short name, parent ID, file lengths, and creation and modification dates. A user with write access can modify the contents of the directory, add and delete directories and files, and modify data within a file.

Another type of AFP access control preserves data integrity by controlling a user's access to a file in use by another workstation. When opening a file, a user can specify **deny modes** (as opposed to access modes). Thus subsequent users trying to open that file can be denied read, read-write, or write access.

The deny modes prevent users from accessing information while it is being changed by another user. They also prevent applications from damaging each other's files by modifying the same version simultaneously.

Overview of AFP calls

AFP calls are the commands the workstation sends to the file server. The following sections describe the calls, grouped by the entity they address. These groups include server calls, volume calls, directory calls, file calls, combined directory-file calls, and fork calls. For detailed information on the inputs and outputs required and the results of these calls, refer to *Inside AppleTalk*.

Server calls

A workstation uses server calls to log on to the file server and to open and close a session (see *Table 4-5*).

■ **Table 4-5** Server calls

Call	Function
FPGetSrvrInfo	Obtains descriptive information about the server
FPGetSrvrParms	Retrieves file server parameters
FPLogin	Establishes a session with a server, specifies the AFP version and user authentication method to use
FPLoginCont	Continues the log-on and user authentication process begun by FPLogin
FPLogout	Terminates a session with a server
FPMapID	Maps a user ID or group ID to a user name or group name
FPMapName	Maps a user name or group name to a user ID or group ID
FPChangePassword	Allows users to change their passwords
FPGetUserInfo	Retrieves information about a user

Volume calls

Volume calls permit the workstation to gain access to or to get information about a specific volume (see *Table 4-6*).

■ **Table 4-6** Volume calls

Call	Function
FPOpenVol	Makes a volume available to a workstation
FPCloseVol	Informs a server that a workstation will no longer use a volume
FPGetVolParms	Retrieves parameters for a volume
FPSetVolParms	Sets the backup date for a volume
FPFlush	Writes to disk any modified data from a volume

Directory calls

The directory calls enable a workstation to create a new directory or access an existing one (see *Table 4-7*).

■ **Table 4-7** Directory calls

Call	Function
FPSetDirParms	Sets parameters for a directory
FPOpenDir	Opens a directory
FPCloseDir	Closes a directory
FPEnumerate	Lists the contents of a directory
FPCreateDir	Creates a new directory

File calls

Using the file calls, a workstation can create new files or modify existing file parameters (see *Table 4-8*).

■ **Table 4-8** File calls

Call	Function
FPSetFileParms	Sets parameters for a file
FPCreateFile	Creates a new file
FPCopyFile	Copies a file from one location to another on the same file server

Combined directory-file calls

The combined directory-file calls manage both files and directories without requiring the user to specify if the CNode is a file or directory (see *Table 4-9*).

■ **Table 4-9** Combined directory-file calls

Call	Function
FPGetFileDirParms	Retrieves parameters for a file or directory
FPSetFileDirParms	Sets parameters for a file or directory
FPRename	Renames a file or directory
FPDelete	Deletes a file or directory
FPMoveAndRename	Moves a file or directory to another location on the same volume and optionally renames it

Fork calls

The fork calls allow the user to access and manipulate a file fork (see *Table 4-10*).

■ **Table 4-10** Fork calls

Call	Function
FPGetForkParms	Retrieves parameters for a fork
FPSetForkParms	Sets parameters for a fork
FPOpenFork	Opens an existing file's data or resource fork
FPRead	Reads the contents of a fork
FPWrite	Writes to a fork
FPFlushFork	Writes to disk any of the fork's data that is in the server's buffer
FPByteRangeLock	Prevents other users from reading or writing data in part of a fork
FPCloseFork	Closes an open fork

AFP interface to the Macintosh desktop

For file server volumes, AFP provides an interface that replaces the Macintosh Finder's direct use of the desktop file with a shared Desktop database maintained by the server. This interface is necessary because the desktop file was designed for a stand-alone environment and does not allow multiple users to read and write simultaneously.

Basically, the Desktop database performs three functions:

- It associates documents and applications with specific icons and stores the icon bitmaps.
- It provides a search mechanism used to locate the appropriate application when a user opens a document.
- It links text comments with files and directories.

For the Desktop database to accomplish these tasks, the AFP interface provides calls that correspond to each function (see *Table 4-11*).

- **Table 4-11** Desktop database calls

Call	Definition
FPAddIcon	Adds an icon bitmap to the Desktop database
FPGetIcon	Retrieves the bitmap for a given icon
FPGetIconInfo	Retrieves an icon's description
FPAddAPPL	Adds mapping information for an application
FPRemoveAPPL	Removes mapping information for an application
FPGetAPPL	Returns the appropriate application to use for a particular document
FPAddComment	Stores a comment with a file or directory
FPRemoveComment	Removes a comment associated with a file or directory
FPGetComment	Retrieves a comment for a file or directory
FPOpenDT	Opens the Desktop database on a specific volume
FPCloseDT	Informs a server that a workstation no longer needs the volume's Desktop database

PostScript

PostScript is the document representation/page description protocol used for communicating with LaserWriter printers. For more information on PostScript, refer to the Adobe Systems publication *PostScript Language Reference Manual* and the Apple publication *LaserWriter Reference*.

AppleTalk Protocols: A review

Chapter 4 introduced the AppleTalk protocols, discussing the features of each and how they work together. The LocalTalk Link Access Protocol (LLAP) provides best-effort delivery of information between nodes on a single network. LLAP manages data encapsulation and provides link access for transmitting and receiving frames. The AppleTalk Address Resolution Protocol (AARP) reconciles addressing discrepancies in networks that support more than one set of protocols.

The Datagram Delivery Protocol (DDP) handles socket-to-socket delivery of packets to nodes on an internet. The Routing Table Maintenance Protocol (RTMP) allows internet routers to dynamically discover routes to networks in an internet. The AppleTalk Echo Protocol (AEP) allows a node to send datagrams to any other node on the network and receive an echoed reply.

The Name Binding Protocol (NBP) converts device names into network addresses. The Zone Information Protocol (ZIP) maintains an internet-wide mapping of networks to zone names.

The AppleTalk Transaction Protocol (ATP) provides loss-free transaction service between sockets. The Printer Access Protocol (PAP) enables communications between workstations and print servers. The AppleTalk Session Protocol (ASP) handles session establishment, maintenanace and teardown, along with request sequencing. The AppleTalk Data Stream Protocol (ADSP) provides reliable, byte stream service between any two sockets on an AppleTalk internet. The AppleTalk Filing Protocol (AFP) allows workstations to share files that reside on a shared resource.

Chapter 5 discusses the AppleTalk Manager, which is a set of AppleTalk drivers that implement the AppleTalk protocols on the Macintosh family of computers.

Chapter 5 **The AppleTalk Manager**

MACINTOSH DEVELOPERS have access to the AppleTalk protocols
via the AppleTalk Manager, which is a set of software drivers that implement
the AppleTalk protocols in the Macintosh family of computers. Equivalent
software exists for the Apple II family and MS-DOS workstations to manage
the AppleTalk protocols, but this chapter focuses on the Macintosh device
drivers. Macintosh applications make use of the AppleTalk protocols by
invoking routines or making calls to the AppleTalk Manager. ■

The AppleTalk Manager is a set of **device drivers** that allow Macintosh programs to send and receive information via an AppleTalk network system.

The AppleTalk protocols are implemented by separate device drivers, which are software modules that handle the details of interaction with a hardware device or other software modules. Drivers are provided as common modules, so that each application need not contain the functionality of the drivers. The AppleTalk drivers primarily interact with the corresponding drivers in other nodes on an AppleTalk internet.

The AppleTalk Manager consists of

- the .MPP driver, which implements LLAP, DDP, AEP, NBP, and part of RTMP

- the .ATP driver, which implements ATP

- the .XPP driver, which implements ASP and a small part of AFP

- high-level language interfaces to the drivers

AppleTalk drivers

The AppleTalk drivers, called .MPP, .ATP, and .XPP, (see *Figure 5-1*) are resources that can be opened and used by an application.

A Macintosh connected to an AppleTalk network with LocalTalk communicates via Channel B of the Serial Communication Controller (SCC). On most Macintosh models, the .MPP, .ATP, and .XPP drivers are kept in ROM. If the drivers are not in ROM, the AppleTalk Manager software is read from disk and loaded into the system heap.

In most cases, the AppleTalk drivers are opened at System startup time. However, the AppleTalk Manager provides high-level language routines to open the .MPP, .ATP, and .XPP drivers to load the AppleTalk code at times other than System startup. While close calls can shut down the drivers, using them is highly discouraged because they also disconnect other coresident programs from AppleTalk.

Most routines can run synchronously or asynchronously. Within an application, a synchronous routine is completed before control returns to the application. An asynchronous routine permits the application to continue processing while the routine is running.

■ **Figure 5-1** AppleTalk drivers

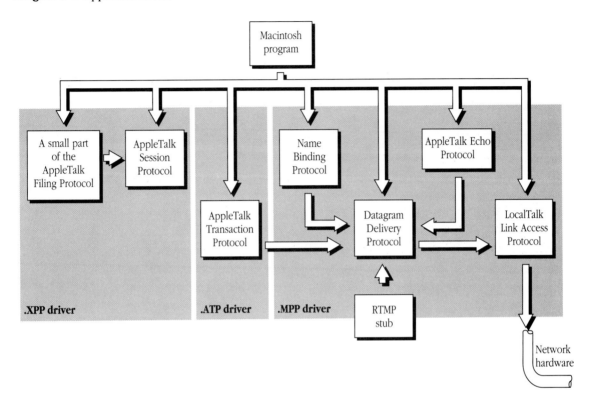

The .MPP driver

The .MPP driver contains code to implement LLAP, DDP, AEP, and NBP as well as the RTMP stub, a subset of RTMP code used by nonrouter nodes. The driver also contains separate code resources that are loaded when an NBP name is registered or looked up.

The .ATP driver

The .ATP driver implements ATP, which provides a reliable loss-free transport service. ATP delivers data through transaction requests and transaction responses.

The .XPP driver

The .XPP (Extended Protocol Package) driver implements the workstation side of ASP and a small portion of the workstation side of AFP.

The latter implementation provides a mechanism for the workstation to send AFP commands to the file server. Other software, separate from the .XPP driver, translates native file system calls to AFP calls.

A workstation application makes a series of calls to .XPP, which the .XPP driver maps to AFP calls. This mapping is usually a simple one-to-one process, whereby one .XPP call is translated into one AFP call, occurring without the driver interpreting the data. There are two exceptions: in the first case, the .XPP driver may break up large FPRead calls; in the second, FPWrite calls may be broken into multiple AFP calls.

Variable resources

The maximum number of AppleTalk resources allowed, such as sockets, concurrently active commands, and protocol handlers, varies for the different Macintosh models. Also, these limits are different if a workstation has AppleShare server software installed. For details on these limits, see *Inside Macintosh, Volume V,* Chapter 28, "The AppleTalk Manager," which contains a chart that lists the resources available for Macintosh Plus, Macintosh SE, and Macintosh II computers.

Calling the AppleTalk Manager from high-level languages

A parameter-block-style interface allows high-level language programs to make calls to the AppleTalk Manager. This interface passes information from an application to the AppleTalk Manager in **parameter blocks,** which are data structures in the heap or stack areas of memory.

Many AppleTalk Manager routines may run either synchronously (meaning that the application cannot continue until the routine is completed) or asynchronously (meaning that the application is free to perform other tasks while the routine is running).

When an application calls an AppleTalk Manager routine asynchronously, an I/O request is placed into the appropriate driver's I/O queue, and control can return to the calling program before the actual I/O is completed. Requests are taken from the queue and are processed one at a time, while the calling program is free to work on other tasks.

Routines that can be run asynchronously are passed a Boolean parameter called `async`. When `async` is TRUE, the call is asynchronous; otherwise, the routine is synchronous. Asynchronous calls return control to the caller with result code `noErr` as soon as they are queued to the driver. To determine when the call is actually completed, a completion routine may be used or the ioResult field may be polled; the ioResult field is set to 1 when the call is made and receives the actual result code upon completion.

Most routines return an integer result code of type `OSErr`. Result codes are generated by the AppleTalk Manager as well as from other parts of the Operating System. With asynchronous calls, the caller may pass a completion routine pointer in the parameter block, designating a routine to run upon completion of the call.

Summary of high-level language calls

All AppleTalk calls can be made from assembly language programs or high-level language programs. The general syntax of AppleTalk calls made from Pascal is

```
FUNCTION MPPCall (pbPtr: Ptr; asyncFlag: BOOLEAN) : OSErr;
```

AppleTalk calls made from C follow this form:

```
OSerr MPPCall (pbPtr, asyncflag)

mppPBPtr  pbPtr;

Boolean  asyncflag;
```

For Pascal or C calls, *MPPCall* represents any .MPP, .ATP, or .XPP call, `pbPtr` points to a parameter block, and `asyncFlag` is TRUE if the call is asynchronous.

The interface defines three parameter block types, one each for .MPP, .ATP, and .XPP. The caller fills in fields of the parameter block and issues the appropriate call. The interface then issues the actual driver call.

The alternate Pascal interface, available before this parameter block-style interface became available, can still be used. For complete descriptions of the calls available from both interfaces, refer to *Inside Macintosh, Volume II,* Chapter 10, and *Volume V,* Chapter 28.

Building data structures

The high-level language interface provides a number of routines for building data structures (see *Table 5-1*) because certain assembly-language structures are problematic for high-level languages to construct and interpret. These data structures include the write data structures for LLAP and DDP, NBP entity structures and names table entries, and the buffer data structure (BDS) used for ATP calls. For details of the routines and descriptions of the data structures, refer to *Inside Macintosh, Volume II,* Chapter 10, and *Volume V,* Chapter 28.

■ **Table 5-1** Data structure routines

Routine	Function
BuildLAPwds	Builds a single-element write data structure LAP WDS
BuildDDPwds	Builds a single-element write data structure DDP WDS
NBPSetEntity	Builds an NBP entity structure
NBPSetNTE	Builds an NBP names table entry
NBPExtract	Extracts an NBP entity name from a lookup response buffer
GetBridgeAddress	Returns a router address, or zero
BuildBDS	Builds a buffer data structure for ATP calls

Calling the AppleTalk Manager from assembly language

An assembly-language program can make calls directly to the AppleTalk drivers. Complete descriptions of these routines and the fields required by each can be found in *Inside Macintosh, Volume II,* Chapter 10 and *Volume V,* Chapter 28.

The AppleTalk Manager: A review

The AppleTalk Manager consists of three drivers: .MPP, .ATP, and .XPP. The .MPP driver implements LLAP, DDP, AEP, and NBP, as well as part of RTMP used by nonrouter nodes. The .ATP driver implements ATP. The .XPP driver implements ASP and part of AFP.

A parameter block-style interface allows high-level language programs to make calls to the AppleTalk Manager. Assembly-language programs can call the AppleTalk Manager directly.

Appendixes

Appendix A **Related Apple Publications**

APPENDIX A is a guide to related Apple publications. The guide contains the publications relevant to the information in the *AppleTalk Network System Overview*. The publications are listed by title below.

Apple File Exchange Technical Reference

AppleShare File Server Administrator's Guide

AppleShare File Server User's Guide

AppleShare PC User's Guide

AppleShare Print Server Administrator's Guide

AppleShare Print Server User's Guide

Asynchronous LaserWriter Driver Developer's Guide

EtherTalk and Alternate AppleTalk Connections Reference

EtherTalk Interface Card

EtherTalk User's Guide

Human Interface Guidelines

Inside AppleTalk

Inside Macintosh

Inter•Poll Network Administrator's Guide

LocalTalk Cable System Owner's Guide

LocalTalk PC Card Owner's Guide

Print Spooling in an AppleTalk Network

Script Manager Developer's Package

Software Applications in a Shared Environment

Speaking of Networks: An Expanded Glossary of Networking Terms ■

Publications guide

This guide lists each publication, identifies the publication's primary audience, and briefly describes its contents.

Apple File Exchange Technical Reference

For developers who wish to write file conversion routines, known as translators, that are used by Apple File Exchange for moving files between different kinds of computers.

AppleShare File Server Administrator's Guide

For AppleShare file server administrators. Describes AppleShare, shows how to set up the file server and workstations, and summarizes maintenance and troubleshooting procedures.

AppleShare File Server User's Guide

For AppleShare file server users from Macintosh workstations. Describes AppleShare, shows how to set up the workstation, tells how to access and use the file server, and summarizes troubleshooting procedures.

AppleShare PC User's Guide

For AppleShare file server users from PC workstations. Describes AppleShare and AppleShare PC, shows how to set up the PC workstation, tells how to use AppleShare PC to access the file server, and summarizes troubleshooting procedures.

AppleShare Print Server Administrator's Guide

For administrators of an AppleShare print server. Explains how to set up a Macintosh as an AppleShare print server, describes how to use AppleShare to manage printing, provides troubleshooting guidelines, and contains the *AppleShare Print Server User's Guide.*

AppleShare Print Server User's Guide

For anyone using an AppleShare print server. Discusses the print server, and explains how to install and access an AppleShare print server from a workstation.

Asynchronous LaserWriter Driver Developer's Guide

For developers creating scripts for the Asynchronous LaserWriter driver to permit a Macintosh and LaserWriter to communicate using asynchronous connections. Details the Asynchronous Connection Language (ACL) used to write Asynchronous LaserWriter driver scripts. Includes an installation disk with the Asynchronous LaserWriter driver, other necessary system/installation files, and several ACL files for Hayes compatible modems and other connection methods.

EtherTalk and Alternate AppleTalk Connections Reference

For software developers creating an alternative AppleTalk implementation or an Ethernet application in conjunction with the Macintosh operating system. Discusses AppleTalk and EtherTalk software, explains the LAP Manager and the AppleTalk Address Resolution Protocol, and describes the EtherTalk driver and EtherTalk Interface card.

EtherTalk Interface Card

For anyone connecting a Macintosh II to an Ethernet network using the EtherTalk Interface Card. Explains how to install and connect the EtherTalk Interface card.

EtherTalk User's Guide

For anyone connecting a Macintosh II to an Ethernet network using EtherTalk. Explains how to access and use EtherTalk and gives some troubleshooting guidelines.

Human Interface Guidelines

For software developers designing applications consistent with the Apple Desktop Interface. Provides design issues to consider for developing user-friendly applications, describes the elements of and philosophy behind the Desktop Interface, and details the element specifications.

Inside AppleTalk

For developers creating applications compatible with AppleTalk features, or for anyone wishing to understand AppleTalk network technology in detail. Provides an overview of the AppleTalk network system, details the network protocols, gives electrical specifications.

Inside Macintosh

For developers creating software for any Macintosh computers. The five-volume set includes user interface guidelines, complete descriptions of routines available for applications to call, and hardware information. Volumes I, II, and III give information on the Macintosh 128K, 512K, and XL computers. Volume IV is an update to the first three volumes and includes information on the Macintosh Plus and 512K enhanced computers. Volume V is an update to the first four volumes and gives information on the Macintosh SE and Macintosh II computers.

Inter•Poll Network Administrator's Guide

For AppleTalk network administrators using the Inter•Poll network diagnostics tool. Gives an overview of Inter•Poll, discusses AppleTalk network system concepts, and explains how to use Inter•Poll for creating network maps and for troubleshooting and maintaining an AppleTalk network.

LaserWriter Reference

For developers or experienced users wanting information on the hardware and firmware features of the LaserWriter, LaserWriter Plus, LaserWriter IINT, and LaserWriter IINTX printers. Describes the operating modes and special capabilities of these printers as well as the hardware and software interfaces of these printers to the host computer.

LocalTalk Cable System Owner's Guide

For anyone connecting an AppleTalk network system with LocalTalk cables. Shows how to set up, add to, and change a network and describes troubleshooting procedures.

LocalTalk PC Card Owner's Guide

For PC users connecting to an AppleTalk network. Covers how to install the LocalTalk PC Card, how to print to LaserWriters from a PC, and how to specify commands from menus or the DOS prompt.

Print Spooling in an AppleTalk Network

For developers creating print spoolers for an AppleTalk network or writing code for PostScript printers. Discusses print spooling in an AppleTalk network, provides architectural specifications of the protocols used with print spooling, and explains the PostScript comment conventions used with AppleTalk print spooler/servers that service PostScript printers.

Script Manager Developer's Package

For software developers creating Script Manager compatible applications. Briefly describes the Script Manager, gives some methods for testing applications for Script Manager compatibility, lists hints and recommendations for writing or modifying applications for Script Manager compatibility, and includes usage notes for the KanjiTalk™ interface and the Arabic Interface System. Also includes four disks: two Macintosh System Tools disks, one each for Arabic and Japanese, that contain system tools configured to work with KanjiTalk and the Arabic Interface System; a Kanji font disk with the fonts needed by KanjiTalk; and the *Script Manager Interfaces* disk that provides the MPW™ Assembly, C, and Pascal interfaces to the Script Manager.

Software Applications in a Shared Environment

For developers creating applications to be used in shared environments, multi-user applications, or multi-launch applications. Discusses shared environments and network application development, gives guidelines for network programming and becoming network aware, and describes the new Macintosh Hierarchical File System (HFS) calls that support shared environments.

Speaking of Networks: An Expanded Glossary of Networking Terms

For anyone wanting a comprehensive glossary of networking terms. Each definition begins with an introductory description of the term, followed by a more technical discussion if necessary.

Appendix B Developer Guidelines for International Distribution

WHETHER DEVELOPING network or application software, programmers may wish to examine the potential international market for their products. This appendix presents issues to consider when developing a product that is easily localized; that is, one that can be adapted for use in different countries. ■

Localizability vs. localization

Localization is the process of adapting an application to a specific language or country. When certain functions within an application depend upon the language spoken in its country of origin, the application requires extensive modifications to be adapted for use in another country's language. An application's localizability measures how easily it can be localized.

Application design requires careful forethought to obtain a high degree of localizability, as opposed to developing a highly localized product. This process is essential to efficiently and successfully market applications internationally. Issues to consider include language differences, local units of measure and time/date formats, paper sizes, and variations in keyboards or character sets.

General localizability guidelines

Text characters vary among languages, as do spacing, punctuation, word order, and format style. With non-Roman writing systems, the text direction differs from that of Roman languages, which are usually written and read from left to right. Arabic is read right to left, then top to bottom, and other languages follow different patterns. Even countries that use the same language may use different measurement units or time formats. For example, the United States and the United Kingdom use some different measurement units, and variations occur in the English language versions used.

To ensure easy localization, avoid placing country- or language-specific information in the application's code. Rather, such information should be stored as **resources,** which can be adapted or substituted without modifying the code.

The International Utilities Package, in the Macintosh System Resource File, and the Script Manager (See *"The Script Manager"*) contain routines that aid in developing applications that are country- and language-independent. Additionally, interfaces are available to help adapt applications to non-Roman languages, such as Japanese (KanjiTalk), Chinese (Hanze), Korean (HangulTalk™), and Arabic.

The Macintosh User Interface Toolbox software helps construct applications that conform to the standard Macintosh user interface. The TextEdit routines in the Toolbox handle basic text formatting and editing, and applications can access these routines to ensure compatibility with the user interface. TextEdit automatically uses the Script Manager for non-Roman scripts.

International text differences

All hard-coded text characteristics are potentially problematic for international products. Stipulating these characteristics as part of the code requires editing the application to adapt it for another language. A language's characteristics include:

- alphabet size
- punctuation rules
- word order
- context form
- text direction
- minimum font size for legibility

Not all alphabets have the same number of characters. English, for example, has 26 characters, German has 30, and Japanese contains more than 40,000. Translation from English makes most text strings longer. Thus, a text string fixed to a length adequate for English may be too short for that of another language. Similarly, menu titles widen when translated and may move too far right or even off the screen.

   Another concern is character size. One-byte code sufficiently stores a Roman character, whereas large character sets, such as Japanese, require two-byte codes. Large characters also need higher resolution for legibility. To be readable, the Japanese system font must allow for 16-by-16 pixel characters.

   Punctuation rules and word order change in different languages. In Spanish, questions begin and end with a question mark, with the beginning symbol upside down (¿Qué?). Adjective and noun positions may reverse, as "big house" translates to "casa grande."

   Contextual forms stem from letters appearing differently depending on position. For instance, an Arabic letter has one positional form when it stands alone, or it may link to a preceding or following letter (or both) resulting in another form. Ligatures are specific letters that join together when they occur in the proper context. Some examples of English ligatures are "æ" and "œ," which are different from the individual letters.

   Text direction varies from standard Roman left-to-right-then-top-to-bottom order (see *Figure B-1*). Arabic is read right to left, then top to bottom, and other languages follow different patterns.

■ **Figure B-1** Different text directions

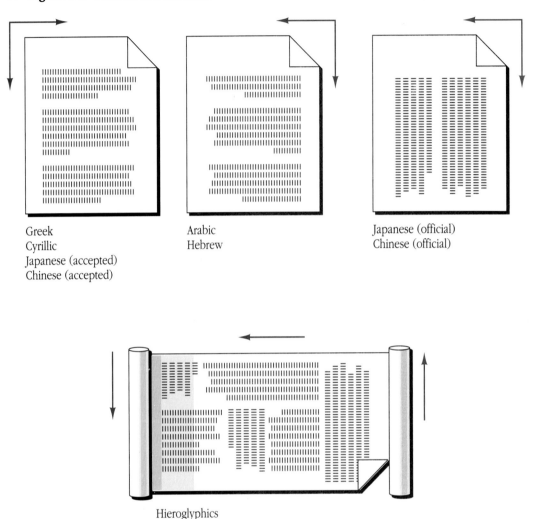

Greek
Cyrillic
Japanese (accepted)
Chinese (accepted)

Arabic
Hebrew

Japanese (official)
Chinese (official)

Hieroglyphics

International format differences

International format differences also affect the display of times, dates, currency symbols, and numeric representations (see *Table B-1*).

■ **Table B-1** Standard international formats

	United States	United Kingdom	Italy	France
Numbers	1,234.56	1,234.56	1.234,56	1234.56
Currency	$0.23	£0.23	L. 0,23	0,23 F
	($0.45)	(£0.45)	L. -0,45	-0,45 F
	$345.00	£345	L. 345	345 F
Time	9:05 AM	09:05	9:05	9:05
	11:30 AM	11:30	11:30	11:30
	11:20 PM	23:20	23:20	23:20
	11:20:09 PM	23:20:09	23:20:09	23:20:09
Short date	12/22/87	22/12/1987	22-12-1987	22.12.87
	2/1/88	01/02/1988	1-02-1988	1.02.88

Units of measure differ from country to country as well. Applications that use measurements, such as a ruler for setting margins and tabs, need to allow different measurement systems. Similarly, standards for paper size vary among countries, so applications should not assume the U.S. standard of letter or legal size paper.

The International Utilities Package

The International Utilities Package facilitates developing country-independent applications. This package contains routines for formatting dates and times and comparing text strings in ways that are appropriate to the country where the application is used. Also included is a routine that tests whether or not to use the metric system.

The routines access country-dependent information stored as resources separately from the application code allowing other applications to gain access to these resources. The International Utilities Package is helpful when developing applications that use:

■ a non-Roman writing system

■ non-English date or time formats

■ routines that compare text strings containing accented characters

For a complete description of the International Utilities Package, refer to *Inside Macintosh, Volume I,* Chapter 19, and *Volume V,* Chapter 16.

International resources

The system resource file released in each country contains the standard international resources for that country. Country-dependent information is stored in the resources of type 'itl0', 'itl1', 'itl2', 'itlb', and 'itlc'.

Resources 'itl0' and 'itl1' correspond to the older versions named 'INTL' 0 and 'INTL' 1. They contain the formats for numbers, currency, time, short dates, and long dates, a routine for localizing string comparisons; they also indicate whether or not to use the metric system. The 'itl2' resource holds sorting procedures.

The International Utilities Package works with the Script Manager to support multiple formats for the same system by adding multiple international script resources. Resource 'itlb' is a script bundle resource that identifies which keyboard and international formats to use. Resource 'itlc' determines the system script.

International resources may be stored in an application's or a document's resource file to override those in the system resource file. This way, the application or document will always access the correct resource file, even if it is used on a Macintosh configured for another country.

Using the International Utilities Package

The International Utilities Package is automatically read into memory from the system resource file when one of its routines is called (see *Table B-2*). When a routine needs to gain access to an international resource, it asks the **Resource Manager** to read the resource into memory.

◘ **Table B-2** International Utilities Package routines

Routine	Function
IUDateString	Returns the short date, long date, or abbreviated long date
IUDatePString	Returns the date, formatted as specified by a given resource
IUTimeString	Returns the time, formatted as specified by 'itl0'
IUTimePString	Returns the time, formatted as specified by a given resource
IUMetric	Indicates whether to use the metric system
IUGetIntl	Returns a handle to the resource 'itl0', 'itl1', or 'itl2'
IUSetIntl	Sets the international resource 'INTL' 0 or 1 to specified data
IUCompString	Compares two Pascal strings, using primary and secondary ordering
IUMagString	Compares two text strings, using primary and secondary ordering
IUEqualString	Compares two Pascal strings, using primary ordering only
IUMagIDString	Compares two text strings, using primary ordering only

By giving the resource handle, some routines permit formatting information to come from a designated resource. This means a routine can access an international resource in a document's or application's resource file when the file is closed. The routines and parameters are detailed in *Inside Macintosh, Volume I,* Chapter 19, and *Volume V,* Chapter 16.

The Script Manager

The **Script Manager** contains general text manipulation routines that let applications function correctly with non-Roman languages, such as Japanese and Arabic, as well as Roman alphabets like English, French, and German. Compatibility with the Script Manager is important for ensuring that applications are generic, thus enabling a Macintosh application to work with different scripts. The Script Manager works with **Script Interface Systems,** which contain the rules for a specific writing method. The Script Manager

- provides standard, easy to use tools for manipulating ordinary text
- facilitates translating an application to another writing system

A **script** is a writing system. Roman scripts are writing systems whose alphabets evolved from Latin. Roman languages generally contain less than 256 characters, and the characters are relatively independent of each other. Non-Roman scripts have various different characteristics.

Script Interface Systems

The Script Manager calls a Script Interface System to perform specific procedure calls for a given script. Calls typically move from the application through the Script Manager to the Script Interface System, and back (see *Figure B-2*).

A separate Script Interface System is required for each script an application uses. Macintosh computers normally use the Roman script, so the Roman Interface System (RIS) is in the System file or in ROM for some models. Other Script Interface Systems are the Kanji Interface System (KIS), or KanjiTalk, for Japanese, the Arabic Interface System (AIS), HangulTalk for Korean, and the Hanze Interface System (HIS) for Chinese.

■ **Figure B-2** Call procedure

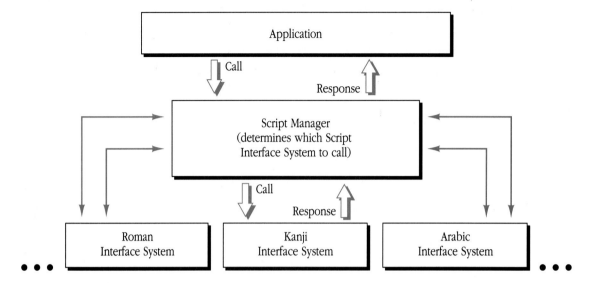

Scripts are available for many languages with each Script Interface System providing:

■ fonts for the language

■ keyboard mapping tables

■ routines to handle character input, conversion, sorting, and text manipulation

■ a desk accessory utility for system maintenance and control

Up to 64 separate Script Interface Systems can be installed at one time on the Macintosh, allowing an application to switch to different scripts. Every available script has a unique identification number, which the Script Manager checks to determine the script in use.

Script Manager routines

The Script Manager routines extend the Macintosh's text manipulation capabilities beyond any implicit assumptions that would limit it to Roman scripts. These limitations occur because of:

■ character set size

■ writing direction

■ context dependence

■ word demarcation

■ text justification

Large character sets may require two-byte codes for storage. Script Manager routines permit applications to run regardless of whether one- or two-byte codes are being used.

The Script Manager provides the capability to write from right to left, as required by Arabic, Hebrew, and other languages, and to mix writing directions within lines and blocks of text. This allows, for example, an English phrase to appear in lines of Arabic text, with both languages reading in appropriate directions. The routines also accommodate context dependent languages, in which ligatures are formed depending on the preceding and following characters.

Words in Roman scripts are generally delimited by spaces and punctuation marks. Japanese scripts may have no word delimiters, so the Script Manager finds word boundaries using a more sophisticated method.

Text justification in Roman languages is done by increasing the spacing between words. In Arabic, however, extension bars are inserted between joined characters and the spacing between words is increased.

Refer to *Inside Macintosh, Volume V,* Chapter 17, for complete descriptions of the routines. See also the *Script Manager Developer's Package* published by Apple, for information on writing Script Manager compatible applications.

TextEdit

TextEdit is a set of routines and data types that provide basic text editing and formatting capabilities for an application. Using TextEdit routines insures that an application presents a consistent user interface, as all the routines follow the Macintosh User Interface Guidelines.

TextEdit supports these standard features:

- Selecting text with the mouse by clicking and dragging and double-clicking
- Altering the text selection by shift-clicking
- Deselecting text
- Displaying the blinking vertical bar at the insertion point
- Wrapping words, rather than splitting them between lines
- Cutting, copying, and pasting text
- Allowing text attributes such as font, size, style, and color to vary within a single text block

All TextEdit routines are fully compatible with the Script Manager. For more information on TextEdit and complete descriptions of the routines, see *Inside Macintosh.*

Guidelines

This list summarizes the guidelines to use when developing an easily localizable product:

- Follow the recommendations of *Inside Macintosh, Human Interface Guidelines,* and the *Script Manager Developer's Package.*

- Put language- and country-specific information in resources. Avoid hard coding font and text information.

- Be aware that characters may need one or more bytes for storage, and that they may change form depending on context and the text direction may vary.

- Do not assume the use of English text. This means avoiding fixing the alphabet length, punctuation rules, string lengths, word order, and sorting order.

- Do not assume the use of U.S. standards. Avoid fixing units of measure, numeric, time, or date formats, and paper sizes.

- Use TextEdit if possible and the Script Manager for specialized text handling.

- Use the International Utilities Package for country-specific formatting.

Text exchange issues

Text exchange issues concern the different ways text is represented or stored. Text representation changes from font to font and among different languages, and text storage methods vary from computer to computer (see *Figure B-3*). This issue is particularly important when developing applications for use on more than one kind of computer, as files may be stored in various forms.

One difficulty arises when transferring files from one computer to a different type of computer. For example, transferring a file from a Macintosh to a PC requires translating the file because the two computers use different codes to represent the same character. This means file transfer applications need to accommodate character set differences and to perform character mapping.

Another issue involves multisystem applications. To illustrate, an application for a multisystem database allows different types of workstations to access a central database. Similarly, workstations may have to access a file server that is a different type of computer. In either case, a translator at the workstation end converts the files as they come in from the file server or application and translates them to the original form as they are sent back.

■ **Figure B-3** Text exchange

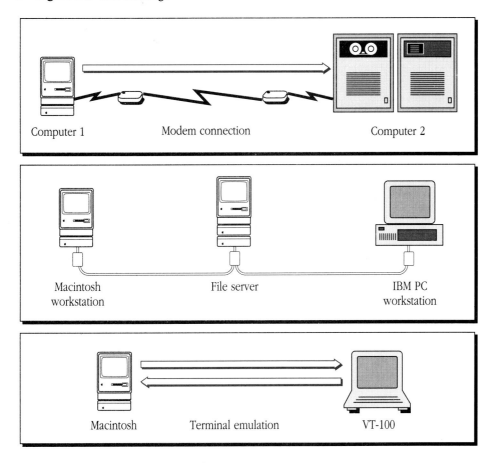

Computer 1   Modem connection   Computer 2

Macintosh   File server   IBM PC
workstation   workstation

Macintosh   Terminal emulation   VT-100

Terminal emulation programs allow a personal computer to imitate the behavior of a specific terminal type. For example, an application may cause a Macintosh computer to emulate a VT-100 terminal. This requires keyboard mapping and character set mapping so that keys pressed on the Macintosh keyboard produce results as though they were typed on a VT-100 keyboard.

The main issues to consider in text exchange are character set and keyboard differences. Applications that will run in different languages or on different computers must undergo a transliteration process, the extent of which depends on the information's initial form and the final form needed.

Key to character translation

For the Macintosh, several steps preclude a character's appearing on the screen when a key is pressed. The steps proceed according to the hardware, or keyboard, and the language used (see *Figure B-4*).

■ **Figure B-4** Key to character translation

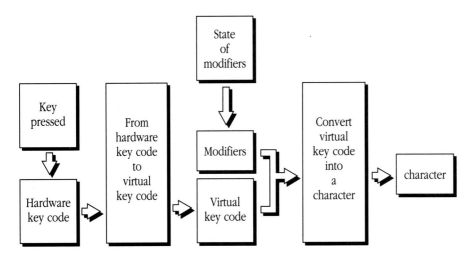

Pressing a key generates a hardware **key code,** also called a raw key code. The hardware key code converts to a virtual key code, such as a Hex value, which varies with the keyboard type. Then, the virtual key code translates to a **character code,** which depends on the language and modifier keys used. The keyboard event message holds the virtual key code and ASCII character generated.

The virtual-key-code-to-character conversion follows a specific character map, as discussed in the next section. The hardware-to-virtual-key-code exchange uses the keyboard mapping scheme, which is covered following the character set discussion. Both keyboard and character mapping schemes reside in the System folder as resources.

Keyboards

Keyboard layout determines how hardware key codes are mapped to virtual key codes. The Macintosh offers six different keyboards:

■ the original Macintosh keyboard, U.S. version

■ the original Macintosh keyboard, international version

■ the Macintosh Plus keyboard

■ the standard ADB keyboard

■ the ISO ADB keyboard

■ the extended ADB keyboard

A pressed key has a corresponding hardware key code. Hardware key codes may be different from virtual key codes, depending on the keyboard used (see *Figure B-5*).

The steps taken to convert key codes vary according to keyboard type. ADB keyboards, whether ISO, standard, or extended type, have different hardware and virtual key codes. The 'KMAP' resource in the System Folder contains the translation map of hardware to virtual key codes for these keyboards. By modifying 'KMAP', key codes can change for these keyboard layouts.

Non-ADB international keyboards undergo a similar translation, with the hardware key codes converted to virtual key codes. Only non-ADB keyboards sold in the U.S. produce the same hardware key codes as virtual key codes, so these keyboards skip the conversion process.

The virtual key codes, along with the modifier key status, transform to characters using the 'KCHR' resource. Both the virtual key code and ASCII character generated are returned in the keyboard event message. In the case of language exceptions, the virtual key codes are first modified, then converted to character values.

■ **Figure B-5** Converting hardware key codes to virtual key codes

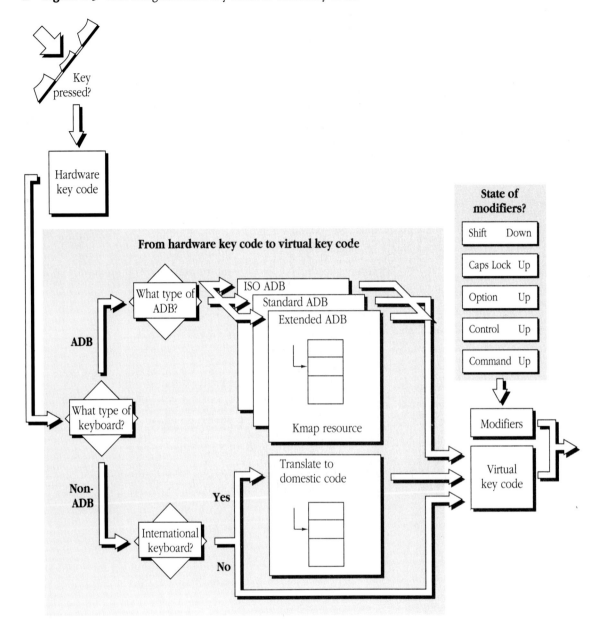

Character sets

Different **character sets** result in text representation changing among countries, computers, and fonts. The Macintosh identifies characters using the extended version of ASCII, while other computers may use various character codes such as 7-bit ASCII, EBCDIC, or ISO 8859. To transliterate between character sets requires code set transformation and language translation.

The Macintosh ASCII codes reside in the 'KCHR' resource of the System File. Characters replace virtual key codes according to the character map in this resource (see *Figure B-6*). Modifying this resource changes the ASCII codes to correspond to different characters, so this resource can be swapped for one of another language.

Any exceptions to a particular language are handled at the virtual key code level. The 'ITLK' resource implements language exceptions by modifying the virtual key code, which is then converted to the character value.

When transliterating between character sets, the process required depends on the source character code set and language. With ASCII representation, ISO substitution sets map character codes of different languages, so translating text becomes a matter of switching character maps. When the source code set differs from the destination code set needed, the transliteration must transform the code set as well as translate the language.

Once the necessary transliteration process is in place, the source text and fonts can be transliterated to the destination text and fonts. Ideally, the end result is translated text, with preserved fonts or other style types, in the appropriate code-set format.

■ **Figure B-6** Converting virtual key codes to characters

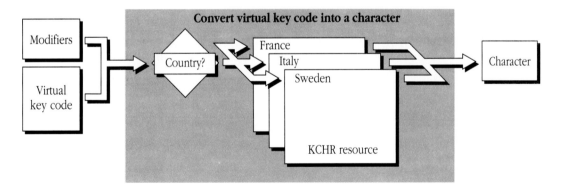

Guidelines

These guidelines summarize considerations for text exchange and keyboard handling:

- Use as much of the local character set as possible. Avoid replacing the entire keyboard layout.

- Substitute character values when possible. If not, substitute virtual key codes. Never attempt to bypass the event record to the keyboard.

- If virtual key codes are substituted, provide a way to reassign functions to different key codes.

- Put all special keyboard requirements or functions in resources.

Glossary

AARP: See **AppleTalk Address Resolution Protocol (AARP).**

access privileges: The privileges given to or withheld from users to open and make changes to a directory and its contents. Through the setting of access privileges, access to the information stored on the file server is controlled.

address mapping table (AMT): A collection of protocol-to-hardware address mapping for each protocol stack that a node supports. The AMT is updated by AARP to ensure that current addressing information is available.

ADSP: See **AppleTalk Data Stream Protocol (ADSP).**

AEP: See **AppleTalk Echo Protocol (AEP).**

AFP: See **AppleTalk Filing Protocol (AFP).**

ALO transaction: See **at-least-once (ALO) transaction.**

AMT: See **address mapping table.**

AppleTalk address: A number that uniquely identifies software processes in an AppleTalk network. The address is composed of the socket number and the identification number of the node (the node ID) containing that socket number. This combination makes a unique address for each socket on a single network.

AppleTalk Address Resolution Protocol (AARP): The protocol that reconciles addressing differences between a data link protocol and the rest of a protocol family. For example, by resolving the differences between an Ethernet addressing scheme and the AppleTalk addressing scheme, AARP facilitates the transport of DDP packets over a high-speed EtherTalk connection.

AppleTalk Data Stream Protocol (ADSP): A connection-oriented protocol that provides a reliable, full-duplex, byte-stream service between any two sockets in an AppleTalk internet. ADSP ensures sequential, duplicate-free delivery of data over its connections.

AppleTalk Echo Protocol (AEP): A simple protocol that allows a node to send a packet to any other node in an AppleTalk internet and to receive an echoed copy of that packet in return.

AppleTalk Filing Protocol (AFP): The presentation-layer protocol that allows users to share data files and application programs that reside in a shared resource, known as a file server.

AppleTalk Manager: An interface to a set of Macintosh device drivers that enable Macintosh programs to send and receive information via an AppleTalk network.

AppleTalk Session Protocol (ASP): A general purpose protocol that uses the services of ATP to provide session establishment, maintenance, and teardown along with request sequencing.

AppleTalk Transaction Protocol (ATP): A transport protocol that provides a loss-free transaction service between sockets. This service allows exchanges between two socket clients in which one client requests the other to perform a particular task and to report the results. ATP binds the request and response together to ensure the reliable exchange of request-response pairs.

ASP: See **AppleTalk Session Protocol (ASP).**

at-least-once (ALO) transaction: An ATP transaction in which the request is repeated until a response is received by the requester or until a maximum retry count is reached. This recovery mechanism ensures that the transaction request is executed at least one time.

ATP: See **AppleTalk Transaction Protocol (ATP).**

attenuation: A decrease in magnitude of current, voltage, or power of a signal in transmission over a medium.

backbone: A central network that connects a number of other, usually lower-speed networks. The backbone network is usually constructed with a high-speed communication medium.

background spooler: A print spooling process that runs in the background on a computer originating a print job.

bandwidth: The capacity of a network to carry information using a particular type of cable (or **medium**), as measured by the maximum number of bits per second (bps) the network can transmit. The higher the bandwidth, the greater the information-carrying capacity of the network and the faster data can be transmitted from one device to another.

broadcast packet: A packet intended to be received by all nodes in a network. In a LocalTalk implementation, broadcast packets are assigned a destination node identification number of 255 ($FF).

broadcast transmission: The transmission of packets intended to be received by all nodes in the network. In a LocalTalk environment, the source sends a lapRTS packet to the broadcast hardware address and then sends the data packet. See **directed transmission.**

bus: A single, shared communication link. Messages are broadcast along the whole bus, and each network device listens for and receives messages directed to its unique address. The physical medium of a LocalTalk network is a twisted-pair bus.

bus topology: A network layout that uses a single cable to connect all the devices in a line that does not connect to itself. On a *bus network*, all devices have equal access to the network and can hear all the messages passed along the cables. Individual devices, however, select and receive only those messages with their specific address.

cable extender: A small plastic adapter with a jack on either end that enables two LocalTalk cables to be connected.

Carrier Sense Multiple Access with Collision Avoidance (CSMA/CA): A technique that allows multiple stations to gain access to a transmission medium (multiple access) by listening until no signals are detected (carrier sense), and then signaling their intent to transmit before transmitting. When contention occurs, transmission is based on a randomly selected order (collision avoidance). The LocalTalk Link Access Protocol, used for node-to-node delivery in a LocalTalk environment, uses the CSMA/CA technique.

character code: A number representing the character that a key or key combination stands for.

character set: All the characters that a computer can use or generate.

client: A software process that makes use of another software process. See **socket client.**

coaxial cable: An electrical cable consisting of a central wire surrounded by a second tubular wire made of braided mesh, both of which have the same center point, or axis, hence the name *coaxial.* Separated from the central wire by insulation, the tubular wire shields electronic impulses travelling across the central wire. In turn, the tubular wire is surrounded by insulation.

connection: An association between two sockets that facilitates the establishment and maintenance of an exclusive dialog between two entities. See **session.**

connection state: The term used to refer collectively to control and state information that is maintained by the two ends of a connection.

connectivity: When two or more devices are joined to a network enabling them to communicate.

connector module: A small box at the end of a LocalTalk connector cable. Network cables plug into the box, which itself is plugged into a workstation or networked peripheral device.

control packets: Messages that do not contain data, but that are used for administrative purposes, such as enquiry, acknowledgment, and notification. Control packets are also used to open and close connections.

CSMA/CA: See **Carrier Sense Multiple Access with Collision Avoidance (CSMA/CA).**

data acceptance: The process by which the receiving end of a connection accepts data from the sending end.

data acknowledgement: A response one device sends to another over the network indicating that the device received a data transmission. The response is a control character or other signal that the receiving device sends to the transmitting device.

data encapsulation/decapsulation: Adding bits required by the protocols to data being sent over a network. Because the bits precede and (usually) follow the data, they are said to surround, or *encapsulate,* the data. As the networking software processes a data packet prior to sending it, the software passes the packet from one protocol layer to the next. The software processes at each layer add bits to the front and sometimes to the back of the packet identifying the various features for which the protocol is responsible. The data is then passed to the next protocol that encapsulates the data, adding its own bits and passing it to the next protocol level. The process of encapsulation continues as the data works its way through all the protocols. The data is then transmitted. The receiving software processes the encapsulated data packet by reversing the procedure. Each layer reads and interprets the bits added by the corresponding layer in the sending software, and then strips off, or *decapsulates*, those bits. As the data packet works its way through the layers of protocols at the receiving device, the decapsulation continues until all the added networking bits are removed from the data.

datagram: A self-contained packet independent of other packets in a data stream. Since a datagram carries its own routing information, its reliable delivery does not depend on earlier exchanges between the source and destination devices. DDP is responsible for delivering AppleTalk transmissions as datagrams.

Datagram Delivery Protocol (DDP): The network-layer protocol that is responsible for the socket-to-socket delivery of datagrams over an AppleTalk internet.

data packets: Messages that contain client data.

data sequencing: In ADSP, a technique that ensures an orderly, sequential flow of data between connections. Each byte sent on the connection in a particular direction has a 32-bit sequence number associated with it.

DDP: See **Datagram Delivery Protocol (DDP).**

deny modes: A set of AFP permissions that establishes what rights should be denied to users attempting to open a file fork that has already been opened by another user.

device driver: Software for using a peripheral hardware device attached to a computer. The driver controls the specific input/output (I/O) to the peripheral. The executive portion of the operating system calls the driver in response to each user I/O call.

directed packet: A packet intended to be received by a single node.

directed transmission: In a LocalTalk environment, the transmission of packets intended to be received by a single node. The source sends a lapRTS packet to the destination; the destination responds with a lapCTS packet; then the source sends the data packet. See **broadcast transmission.**

entity: See **network-visible entity.**

entity name: A name that a network visible entity (NVE) may assign itself. Although not all NVEs have names, NVEs can possess several names (or aliases). An entity name consists of character strings: object, type, and zone.

EtherTalk: Apple's data-link product that allows an AppleTalk network to be connected by Ethernet cables.

EtherTalk Link Access Protocol (ELAP): the link-access protocol used in an EtherTalk network. ELAP is built on top of the standard Ethernet data-link layer.

exactly-once (XO) transaction: An ATP transaction in which the request is delivered only one time, thus protecting against damage that could result from a duplicate transaction.

file server: A computer running a specialized program that provides network users with access to shared disks or other mass storage devices. Through the implementation of access controls, a file server facilitates controlled access to common files and applications.

flow control: Techniques to assure that data moves over the network in a continuous, smooth manner. One flow control technique uses Xon/Xoff control characters to indicate when a transmission is to start and stop (the X standing for transmission). With this technique, as the receiving workstation's buffer approaches its limit, the workstation transmits the off (stop) character to pause the transmission of data. When the buffer again has sufficient space to store received data, the workstation transmits the on (start) character and the transmission resumes.

folder: A container that can hold documents, applications, and other folders on the Desktop. Folders act as subdirectories, keeping files organized in any manner needed by the user.

fork: Macintosh files are divided into two parts know as forks: The data fork is an unstructured finite sequence of data bytes. The resource fork is the part of a file that is accessible through the Macintosh Resource Manager and that contains specialized data used by an application such as menus, fonts, and icons (as well as the application code for an application file).

gateway: An electronic device that separates and manages communication between different types of networks. A gateway is used to connect an AppleTalk protocol-based network to a non-AppleTalk protocol-based system. The gateway serves as a translator between the protocols of the two connected networks.

hardware address: The unique node address that is determined by the physical and data link layers of the network.

Hierarchical File System (HFS): The file system used on Macintosh hard disks and 800K disks.

hop: On a network, each time a datagram passes an internet router enroute to its destination.

internet: One or more networks connected by intelligent nodes referred to as internet routers.

internet address: The address of a socket in an AppleTalk internet. This address is made up of the socket number, the node ID of the node in which the socket is located, and the network number of the network in which the node is located. The internet address provides a unique identifier for any socket in an AppleTalk internet.

internet router: See **router.**

keyboard layout: The mapping of a character code with each key or combination of keys on the keyboard or keypad.

key code: A number that represents one of the keys on the keyboard. The number can represent a symbol that the key can produce even though the symbol is not visible on the keyboard.

LAP Manager: The interface between the higher-level AppleTalk protocols and the various link access protocol implementations in a particular node.

LAN: See **local area network (LAN).**

LLAP: See **LocalTalk Link Access Protocol (LLAP).**

local area network (LAN): A network in one location. A typical local area network is joined by a single transmission cable and is located within a small area, such as a single building or section of a building.

localization: The process of adapting an application to different languages, including converting its user interface to a different script.

LocalTalk: The name for Apple Computer's low-cost connectivity product consisting of cables, connector modules, cable extenders, and other cabling equipment for connecting computer and other devices.

LocalTalk Link Access Protocol (LLAP): The link level protocol that manages node-to-node delivery of data in a LocalTalk environment. LLAP manages bus access, provides a node-addressing mechanism, and controls data transmission and reception, ensuring packet length and integrity.

medium: The physical means used to connect devices on a network. Examples include copper wire, optical fibers, and microwave channels.

name binding: The NBP process by which an entity name is mapped to its internet address.

Name Binding Protocol (NBP): The AppleTalk transport-level protocol that translates a character string name into the internet address of the corresponding socket client. NBP enables AppleTalk protocols to understand user-defined zones and device names by providing and maintaining translation tables that map these names to corresponding socket addresses.

name confirmation: The NBP process that checks and validates the current name binding.

name deletion: The NBP process by which an entity removes its name and internet address from the names directory.

name lookup: The NBP process that binds the entity's name to its internet address.

name registration: The NBP process whereby an entity enters its name and internet address into the names directory.

names directory: A distributed database of entity name-to-entity address maps. The names directory is the union of the individual names tables in all the nodes of an internet.

names table: A table in each node that contains entity name-to-entity internet address mappings of all named network-visible entities in the node.

native file system: Part of a computer's operating system which manages the manipulation of files on a disk or other memory resource that is physically connected to a workstation.

NBP: See **Name Binding Protocol (NBP).**

network: A collection of individually-controlled computers, printers, modems, and other electronic devices interconnected so they can all communicate with each other. Networks also include all the software used to communicate on the network and the wires, cables, connector modules, and other hardware that make the physical connections.

network number: A 16-bit number that uniquely identifies a network in an AppleTalk internet.

network-visible entity: A resource addressable through the network. Typically, the network-visible entity is a socket client for a service available in a node. See **entity name.**

node: A data-link addressable entity on a network.

node ID (node identifier): A number used to uniquely identify each node on a communication medium.

noise resistance: The ability of a cable to keep unwanted outside signals (noise) from interfering with the transmitted signals.

packet: A group of bits, including data and control elements, that is transmitted together as a unit within a frame. The control elements include a source address, a destination address, and possibly error-control information.

packet sequencing: A technique ensuring that packets are received in the correct order. Each ADSP, PAP, and ASP packet carries a sequence number that is checked during packet reception and compared to the expected sequence number. If the numbers match, the packet is accepted.

PAP: See **Printer Access Protocol (PAP).**

parameter block: A data structure used to transfer information between an application and certain operating system routines.

Printer Access Protocol (PAP): The AppleTalk protocol that manages interaction between workstations and print servers. PAP handles connection setup, maintenance, and termination, as well as data transfer.

print server: A hardware or software application (or both) that intercepts printable document files and that interacts with a printer to print the document, freeing the originating computer of this responsibility.

print spooler: See **print server.**

protocols: A set of procedural rules for information exchange over a communication medium. These rules govern the content, format, timing, sequencing, and error control of messages exchanged in a network.

protocol address: The unique address that a node assigns to identify the protocol client that is to receive a packet for a particular protocol stack.

resource: Data or code stored in a file which is manipulated by the Resource Manager.

Resource Manager: Part of the Macintosh Toolbox through which an application accesses various resources that it uses, such as menus, fonts, and icons.

router: An electronic device that connects networks and serves as the key component in extending the datagram delivery mechanism to an internet setting. A router functions as a packet-forwarding agent to allow datagrams to be sent between any two nodes of an internet by using a store-and-forward process. Routers fall into three categories: local routers, half routers, and backbone routers. See also **gateway.**

router ports: The physical hardware ports on a router device.

routing table: A table, resident in each AppleTalk internet router, that serves as a map of the internet, specifying the path and distance (in hops) between the internet router and other networks. Routing tables are used to determine whether and where a router will forward a data packet. RTMP is used to update the routing tables.

Routing Table Maintenance Protocol (RTMP): The AppleTalk protocol used to establish and maintain the routing information that is required by internet routers in order to route datagrams from any source socket to any destination socket in the internet. Using RTMP, internet routers dynamically maintain routing tables to reflect changes in internet topology.

routing tuple: The last part of an RTMP data packet. Routing tuples consist of two values: the destination network number and the distance (in hops) from the sending internet router to the destination network.

RTMP: See **Routing Table Maintenance Protocol (RTMP).**

script: A writing system, such as Cyrillic or Arabic. The English language uses Roman script.

Script Interface System: Special software that supports the display and manipulation of a particular script.

Script Manager: A set of text manipulation routines that lets applications function correctly with non-Roman languages.

server folder: A special folder on each AppleShare file server volume that contains information about the volume, allowing the file server software to recognize the volume as a valid file server volume.

session: A logical connection between two network entities (typically, a workstation and a server) that facilitates establishment and maintenance of an exclusive dialog between the two entities. In an AppleTalk network, ASP can be used to establish, maintain, and tear down sessions; ASP also ensures that commands transmitted during a session are delivered in the same order as they were

sent, and that the results of the commands are conveyed back to the originating entity. See **connection.**

socket: An addressable entity within a node connected to an AppleTalk network; sockets are owned by software processes known as socket clients. AppleTalk sockets are divided into two groups, statically assigned sockets, which are reserved for clients such as AppleTalk core protocols, and dynamically assigned sockets, which are assigned dynamically by DDP upon request from clients in the node.

socket client: A software process or function implemented in a network node.

socket listener: Code provided by the socket client to receive datagrams addressed to the socket.

spooler/server: A combination of hardware and software that stores documents sent to it over a network and manages the printing of the documents on a printer. Spool stands for *simultaneous peripheral operations on line.*

startup volume: An AppleShare file server volume that contains the server application and related files in its server folder. A file server has only one startup volume.

topology: The physical layout of a network, including the cables and devices.

transaction: An exchange of information between a source and a destination client that accomplishes a particular action or result. In an AppleTalk environment, ATP provides a transaction service that enables a sources client's request to be bound to the destination client's response.

transaction request: An ATP packet sent to ask an ATP client to perform an action and to return a response.

transaction response: An ATP packet sent in response to a transaction request, specifying the results of the requested operation.

transceiver: A device that can both transmit and receive data. The term is a combination of the words *transmitter* and *receiver*.

twisted-pair cable: Ordinary telephone wire consisting of two insulated copper strands twisted about each other to reduce outside interference of their signals. Sometimes referred to as telephone twisted pair, or TTP.

user authentication method : Any procedure used by a server and workstation by which the server is convinced of the user's identity.

volume: A file storage unit. Each disk attacked to an AppleShare file server is considered a volume, although some disks may contain multiple volumes.

volume catalog: A tree-structured catalog of the files and directories on a volume.

workstation: The terminal, console, personal computer or other similar device at which a person sits to work on the network.

XO transaction: See **exactly-once transaction.**

ZIP: See **Zone Information Protocol (ZIP).**

ZIT: See **Zone Information Table (ZIT).**

zone: An arbitrary subset of networks within an internet.

Zone Information Protocol (ZIP): The AppleTalk session-layer protocol that is used to maintain an internet-wide mapping of network numbers to zone names; ZIP is used by NBP to determine which networks belong to a zone.

Zone Information Table (ZIT): A complete network number-to-zone name mapping of the internet maintained by each internet router in an AppleTalk internet.

Index

A

AARP. *See* AppleTalk Address Resolution Protocol

accessing
  directories 7, 29–31, 119
  files 7, 28–29, 41, 54, 113–114, 117
  file servers 29–31, 36–42
    from a Macintosh 32, 36–39
    from an Apple II 32, 36, 39–40
    from a PC 32, 40–42
  folders 29–32
  printers 42–49, 65, 95–96
  volumes 29–31, 116

access privileges 7, 29–31. *See also* accessing; directories; file server

ACL. *See* Asynchronous Connection Language

adapter, cable extender 14. *See also* LocalTalk

adding users to an AppleShare file server 34–35

addresses
  'adev' file 19–20
  AppleTalk 20, 22, 61–63, 72–74
  AppleTalk Address Resolution Protocol (AARP) 61–63, 71–74
  assigning 72–73
  broadcast 22
  destination 20

discrepancies, resolving 61–63, 71–74
  Ethernet 20, 63, 72–74
  handling 72–73
  hardware 20, 63, 72–74
  internet 77
  invalid 74
  mapping 20, 63, 72–73, 86–88
  named entities 86–88
  node 20, 63, 67–69
  numeric 85
  packet 73
  printer 43
  protocol 20, 22, 63, 72–74
  removing 74
  router, returning 128
  server's session listening socket (SLS) 113
  socket 76–77
  source 20

addressing schemes 12
address mapping 20, 63, 72–74, 86–88
Address Mapping Table (AMT) 20, 72, 74
Address Resolution Protocol. *See* AppleTalk Address Resolution Protocol
'adev' files 19–20
Admin application. *See* AppleShare Admin application
administering file server 32–36. *See also* file server

administrators
  AppleShare file server and 32–36
  Inter•Poll and 50–53
ADSP. *See* AppleTalk Data Stream Protocol
AEP. *See* AppleTalk Echo Protocol
AFP. *See* AppleTalk Filing Protocol
AFP Translator 113–114. *See also* AppleTalk Filing Protocol
ALO. *See* at-least-once transaction
AMT. *See* Address Mapping Table
Apple CD SC 33
Apple Hard Disk 20 32–33. *See also* hard disk drives
Apple Personal Modem 48. *See also* modem(s)
AppleShare Admin application 33–36
AppleShare file server 28–42. *See also* file server
AppleShare file server software
  AppleShare File Server: Server Administration 32–33
  AppleShare File Server: Server Installer 32
  AppleShare File Server: Workstation Installer, For use with the Macintosh 512K enhanced only 32
  AppleShare File Server: Workstation Installer, For use with the Macintosh Plus, SE, and II 32

163

mapping 87
Name Binding Protocol and
    43, 64–65, 85–88, 113, 128
name-lookup operation 64–65,
    87–88
names information socket 7
name-to-address mapping 87
registration of 87–88
table 87, 128
zone 64–65, 90
Zone Information Protocol
    and 64–65
Name Binding Protocol (NBP) 43,
    64–65, 85–88, 128
description of 85–88
entity names 85–86
function of 43, 64–65, 113
name binding process 86–88
NBP Broadcast Request packets
    88
NBP entity names, extracting
    from lookup response
    buffer 128
NBP entity structures, building
    128
NBP lookup packets 88
NBP tuple 86
on a single network 88
on internets 88
services of 87–88
Zone Information Protocol
    and 65
named addresses 85
named entities 64–65, 85–88
addresses of 86–88
Name Binding Protocol and
    64–65
Zone Information Protocol
    and 64–65
named entities protocols. *See also*
    protocol(s) *or specific*
    protocol

Name Binding Protocol (NBP)
    64–65
Zone Information Protocol
    (ZIP) 64–65, 89–90
name field 86
name-lookup operation 64–65,
    87–88
name registration 87–88
names directory 87
names information socket 87
names table 87, 128
name-to-address mapping 87
naming
devices 64–65
zones 90
native file system 54, 112–113, 126
NBP. *See* Name Binding Protocol
network(s). *See also specific topic*
backbone 78
components of 2–9
definition of 11
dialing in 48
goals of 2–3
history of 1–3
integrity of 50–51
internets 8–9, 16, 37, 64–65,
    74–84, 86–90
introduction to 1–10
LANSTAR 49
mapping 50
performance, monitoring 50
public data 48
searching 51–52
security of 116
services 6–7, 28–49
single 66–71, 88
testing 50–53
topology of 4, 6, 16, 23, 35–36,
    50
troubleshooting 50–53
network administrators
AppleShare file server and
    32–36

Inter•Poll and 50–53
network applications. *See*
    applications
network architecture
attributes of 2–3
layered 61–62
protocol architecture 4–5
network connections. *See*
    AppleTalk Data Stream
    Protocol; cables;
    connections *or specific*
    topic
network control device package
    (EtherTalk Control Panel
    software) 18
network devices. *See* devices *or*
    specific device
network interface cards. *See*
    interface cards
Network Map file (Inter•Poll) 50
network number 77, 89
network protocols 59–122. *See*
    also protocol(s) *or specific*
    protocol
Network Search window
    (Inter•Poll) 51–52
network services 28–49
network-to-zone mapping 90
network-visible entity 85–86
node(s)
addressing 20, 63, 67–69
catalog 115
confirming existence of 83–84
definition of 8
distance between 25
dynamic node ID assignment
    67–68
fair access for 67
ID numbers 67–69, 81
nonrouter 125
number allowed 25